Still Fuel in the Tank. Be the Man You Always Wanted to Be

No More Wasted Years – Take Control, Rekindle Passion, and Own Your Future

BRYCE DOMINIC VALOR

Disclaimer

This book is for informational and educational purposes only. The content is not intended as financial advice or a recommendation for any specific investment or financial strategy. The author does not hold liability for any actions taken based on the information provided. Readers are encouraged to conduct their own research and consult with a licensed financial advisor before making any financial decisions. Personal responsibility is key to all financial outcomes.

ISBN Hardcover: 979-8312935462

ISBN Paperback: 979-8305805642

Brye Dominic Valor represented by
Summit Edge Publishing
c/o IP-Management #5440
Ludwig-Erhard-Str. 18 |20459 Hamburg
Germany

SUMMIT EDGE
PUBLISHING

Table of Contents

Introduction:

Awaken the Possibilities

Life doesn't come with a pause button, does it? Somewhere along the way, as you've been living, working, providing, and striving, you may have looked up one day and thought, *How did I get here? And is this all there is?* That moment—the one you might even feel a little guilty for having—is exactly why this book is here for you.

You're holding these pages because deep down, you know you're meant for more. More energy. More connection. More joy. And it's not just a hollow yearning—it's a call. A call to awaken the possibilities still waiting within you. Whether it's the drive to reignite old passions, find purpose in the relationships that matter most, or create a life that feels both meaningful and fulfilling, this book is here to walk beside you.

I know how precious your time is. In fact, it might be the most valuable resource we have. So before we dive into this journey together, let me say thank you. Thank you for choosing to invest these moments in yourself, your growth, and your future. This book isn't a lecture, and it isn't a quick-fix solution. It's a partner—a guide to help you discover the strength, wisdom, and energy that already exist within you.

What to Expect

This isn't about telling you what's wrong or what needs fixing. It's about unlocking what's already there, waiting for the right tools and focus to thrive. Over the next chapters, you'll explore the profound yet practical steps to rekindle your passion, reclaim your vitality, and redefine your purpose. Together, we'll tackle fears of wasted time, dismantle the myth that it's too late, and guide you toward a life that feels not just good—but extraordinary.

Through powerful stories, psychological insights, and practical tools, you'll learn how to:

- Turn regrets into stepping stones toward your greatest opportunities.
- Rebuild energy and health, starting today.
- Rekindle intimacy in relationships and deepen connections with family and friends.
- Take control of your financial future and align your daily life with your values.

This journey won't be about perfection. It will be about progress. Small, consistent steps that lead to big, life-changing outcomes.

A Personal Word of Gratitude

It takes courage to show up for yourself. In a world that pulls your attention in a thousand directions, you're here, choosing to focus on your growth and future. That decision deserves recognition and gratitude.

Time, as we said, is our most valuable currency. You've decided to invest it here, not just for yourself but for the people you care about—those who look up to you, count on you, and love you.

This book is a way of honoring that choice, giving you the tools to make this investment one that pays dividends for years to come.

You may not realize it yet, but by the end of this journey, you'll be looking back with a sense of pride and purpose, knowing you chose not to settle but to step up. The second act of your life is waiting, and it starts here. Let's begin.

Part 1:
Reignite Your Inner Fire

CHAPTER 1:
THE CLOCK ISN'T TICKING - IT'S STARTING

My Wake-Up Call at 53

It was a crisp January morning, and the sun had barely begun to rise, casting long, soft shadows on the frost-covered ground. The house was silent, save for the faint tick of the clock in the kitchen. I sat at the table, my hands wrapped around a mug of coffee that had long since gone cold. My reflection in the window stared back at me—a face lined with time, wisdom, and perhaps a touch of weariness.

It was my 53rd birthday.

Birthdays used to feel like milestones of excitement—a celebration of what I had achieved and a chance to dream about what was next. But this one was different. This one felt heavy. Instead of looking forward, I found myself looking back, consumed by an unsettling mix of regret and longing.

Reflecting on Dreams Deferred

I thought about the promises I'd made to myself when I was younger. I'd told myself I would write a book—no, several books—by now. I'd dreamed of traveling to places I'd only ever seen in glossy magazine spreads. I'd imagined taking risks, starting ventures, and living boldly. But as I sat there that morning, staring into the murky depths of my untouched coffee, all I could see were the dreams I hadn't pursued.

"What happened?" I whispered to no one in particular.

The answer wasn't simple. Life had happened. Responsibilities had piled up. Bills needed paying, children needed raising, and careers demanded time and attention. Slowly, almost imperceptibly, the dreams I'd once held so tightly slipped to the margins of my life.

But as I sat there, it wasn't just regret that consumed me—it was fear. Fear that those dreams had passed their expiration date. Fear that I'd waited too long. Fear that maybe I didn't have what it took anymore.

The *"What Ifs"* and the Weight of Stagnation

Fear is an insidious companion. It doesn't always roar loudly; often, it sneaks in quietly, filling the spaces between thoughts, whispering doubts that make you question everything. That morning, as I sat in the stillness of my kitchen, fear wasn't just present—it was overwhelming.

"What if it's too late?"

"What if I've wasted too much time to make a change?"

"What if trying now only leads to failure?"

The questions weren't new. They'd been following me for years, a persistent whisper in the back of my mind. But on that birthday, they felt louder, more urgent.

I glanced at the clock on the wall, its steady ticking a cruel reminder of the time that seemed to slip through my fingers faster with each passing year. I'd spent so much of my life focused on doing what I thought I was supposed to do—building a career, raising a family, meeting expectations. And while I was proud of many of those accomplishments, I couldn't shake the feeling that I'd lost touch with the parts of myself that once made me feel alive.

The Ache of Stagnation

Stagnation is a heavy feeling. It's not the same as failure; it's the sense that you're standing still while the world moves on around you. I felt like I was stuck in a life that was comfortable but unfulfilling, predictable but uninspired.

The weight of that realization was almost too much to bear. I thought about the moments I'd let pass me by—the times I'd chosen safety over risk, familiarity over adventure. I thought about the relationships I hadn't nurtured, the hobbies I'd abandoned, the person I'd hoped to become but hadn't.

But even in the midst of that heaviness, there was a small voice inside me—a voice I'd ignored for far too long.

"What if it's not too late?" it whispered.

"What if the best is still ahead?"

Psychological Insights on Life Milestones

What I didn't know then, but have since learned, is that these moments of reflection—the ones that feel heavy and overwhelming—are often the catalysts for profound change. Psychologists have studied the phenomenon of *"life milestones"* extensively, and the findings are both fascinating and encouraging.

Milestone moments like birthdays, retirements, or significant life transitions force us to pause and take stock of where we've been and where we're going. While these moments can feel unsettling, they also provide an opportunity to realign our lives with our values and goals.

Research published in *Psychology Today* highlights how these periods of reflection are essential for growth. They challenge us to confront the stories we've been telling ourselves—stories about who we are, what we're capable of, and what's possible.

That morning at the kitchen table, I didn't have all the answers. But I began to understand that my fear and regret weren't just barriers—they were invitations. Invitations to rewrite my narrative, to step off the path I'd been on and onto one that felt more aligned with who I wanted to be.

A Moment of Clarity

As the sun climbed higher in the sky, flooding the kitchen with light, I made a decision. I didn't need to have everything figured out that day. I didn't need to know exactly what the future would hold. But I did need to start.

That birthday marked the beginning of a new chapter—not because everything changed overnight, but because I chose to believe that change was possible.

Why Time is a Mental Construct

The first time I truly began to understand the idea of *psychological time*, I was sitting in the same kitchen where I'd had my wake-up call at 53. This time, however, I wasn't lost in regret. I was reflecting on something deeper: how much of my fear about wasted time wasn't about time itself, but about how I was choosing to view it.

We often think of time as fixed, don't we? It's this ticking clock we measure our lives by, counting the years, the milestones, the achievements—or the lack of them. But what if time isn't as rigid as we imagine? What if it's less about the numbers on a clock and more about the stories we tell ourselves about those numbers?

Shaped by Stories

Psychological time is the concept that our perception of time isn't governed by the clock but by our thoughts, emotions, and the narratives we create. For years, my story about time was one of scarcity. I'd tell myself that I hadn't done enough, that I'd wasted precious years, that I was running out of time to become the person I wanted to be.

This story wasn't just unhelpful—it was paralyzing. It kept me locked in a cycle of regret and inaction. And I know I'm not alone in this.

Think about it: how often do you catch yourself saying things like, *"It's too late for me,"* or, *"If only I'd started earlier"*? These thoughts don't come from the reality of time; they come from the beliefs we've internalized about what time should mean.

A New Perspective

One day, as I was reading Viktor Frankl's *Man's Search for Meaning*, a line stopped me in my tracks. Frankl wrote, *"When we are no longer able to change a situation, we are challenged to change ourselves."*

Frankl's words hit me like a revelation. I couldn't change the years that had passed, but I could change the way I saw them. I could stop treating time as a thief and start seeing it as a teacher.

The years I'd lived weren't wasted—they were filled with lessons, experiences, and wisdom that could guide me forward. Every mistake I'd made, every dream I'd deferred, every moment I'd thought was lost—they weren't barriers. They were stepping stones.

Reframing Age as an Asset

This shift in perspective didn't just change how I saw time; it changed how I saw myself. For so long, I'd viewed my age as a limitation. I'd look at younger people with their boundless energy and endless opportunities and think, *If only I had their time.*

But what I failed to see was the incredible value of the years I had lived. Age isn't just a number—it's a repository of wisdom, resilience, and perspective. The challenges I'd faced had made me stronger. The experiences I'd had had made me wiser.

I began to think about people who had achieved greatness later in life. Colonel Sanders didn't start KFC until he was in his 60s. Julia Child didn't publish her first cookbook until her late 40s. Grandma Moses didn't start painting until her 70s. These weren't stories of people lamenting lost time. They were stories of people using the fullness of their lives to create something extraordinary.

Their examples reminded me that it's not age that defines us—it's action.

The Power of Rewriting the Narrative

I started to ask myself new questions. Instead of, *"What have I lost?"* I began asking, *"What have I gained?"* Instead of, *"Is it too late?"* I asked, *"What can I do now?"*

These weren't just rhetorical questions. They were practical. They shifted my focus from scarcity to possibility, from regret to action.

Reframing time isn't about ignoring the past; it's about reinterpreting it. It's about seeing the years you've lived not as something to mourn, but as something to build upon.

Insights from Viktor Frankl

Viktor Frankl's experiences during the Holocaust gave him a profound understanding of human resilience and the search for meaning. He wrote, *"Everything can be taken from a man but one thing: the last of the human freedoms—to choose one's attitude in any given set of circumstances, to choose one's own way."*

Frankl's insights taught me that meaning isn't something we find—it's something we create. And that creation isn't bound by time or age. It's bound only by our willingness to act.

In the years since my wake-up call at 53, I've held tightly to Frankl's lessons. They remind me that the power to change my life isn't tied to a calendar. It's tied to the choices I make each day.

A New Relationship with Time

Psychological time isn't fixed. It's fluid, shaped by our beliefs and attitudes. When I stopped seeing time as something that was running out and started seeing it as something that was building up, everything changed.

I realized that every day I lived, I was gaining something—knowledge, experience, perspective—that I could use to create a better future. And that realization wasn't just liberating—it was empowering.

My Transformation

The morning I turned 53 wasn't the end of the story—it was the beginning. In the days and weeks that followed, I found myself returning to the thoughts that had surfaced during those quiet, reflective hours at my kitchen table. But this time, I wasn't just replaying the regrets. I was searching for a way forward.

I realized I had a choice to make: I could continue to dwell on the years I thought I'd lost, or I could begin to see them as preparation for the future I still had the power to create. It wasn't an easy decision, but it was a necessary one.

Rediscovering My Life Goals

The first step in my transformation was to revisit the goals I'd once cherished—the ones I'd tucked away in the back of my mind, thinking there would always be time for them later. I pulled out an old notebook where I'd jotted down dreams from my twenties. The pages were yellowed and creased, but the words still held their power.

Write a book.

Travel to Italy.

Learn to play the guitar.

At first, seeing those goals written out was bittersweet. They felt like artifacts from another life, reminders of a version of myself I'd long since left behind. But as I sat with them, I began to feel something else: a flicker of excitement. These weren't just remnants of the past—they were possibilities for the future.

I realized I didn't need to pursue them all at once. What I needed was to take the first step.

Journaling My Way Forward

To make sense of my swirling thoughts and emotions, I started journaling. Every morning, I'd pour my thoughts onto the page—my fears, my hopes, the doubts that still lingered. Journaling became a lifeline, a way to clarify my goals and confront the beliefs that had been holding me back.

Through this practice, I noticed patterns in my thinking. I'd been telling myself stories about what I could and couldn't do, stories rooted in fear and self-doubt. But as I wrote, I began to challenge those narratives.

"What if it's not too late?"

"What if my experiences have uniquely prepared me for this moment?"

"What if I have everything I need to start again?"

Writing these questions down didn't magically dissolve my fears, but it did create space for a new perspective. It allowed me to imagine a future that wasn't dictated by regret, but by possibility.

Setting Small, Purposeful Goals

Once I'd clarified what I wanted, the next step was to break those dreams into actionable steps. I knew from experience that vague goals like *"write a book"* or *"get in shape"* would only lead to frustration. What I needed were goals that were specific, measurable, and realistic.

This is where the SMART goals framework came into play. SMART stands for Specific, Measurable, Achievable, Relevant, and Time-bound. It's a method I'd heard about for years but had never fully embraced—until now.

Instead of saying, *"I want to write a book,"* I set a goal to write for 30 minutes every morning before starting my day.

Instead of saying, *"I want to get healthy,"* I committed to taking a 20-minute walk every evening.

These small, purposeful actions might not have seemed monumental, but they were enough to create momentum. And as the days turned into weeks, that momentum began to build.

The Power of Gratitude

Another practice that became central to my transformation was gratitude journaling. Every morning, alongside my reflections and goal-setting, I made a point to write down three things I was grateful for.

At first, this felt awkward, even forced. But over time, it shifted my focus. Instead of dwelling on what I thought I lacked, I began to notice the abundance already present in my life.

I was grateful for the support of my family, for the wisdom I'd gained through the years, for the chance to start anew. This simple practice didn't just change my mindset—it changed the way I approached each day.

Finding New Energy

As I committed to these small, purposeful actions, something remarkable began to happen: I felt my energy return. It wasn't just physical energy—it was a deeper sense of vitality, a feeling that I was moving toward something meaningful.

I started to look forward to my morning writing sessions, to my evening walks, to the quiet moments of reflection and gratitude. These routines didn't just fill my days—they gave them purpose.

The Fulfillment of Action

One of the most surprising things I discovered during this process was how fulfilling it was simply to take action. For so long, I'd been paralyzed by the fear of failure, convinced that if I couldn't achieve perfection, it wasn't worth trying.

But what I realized was that progress, no matter how small, was its own reward. Each step I took reinforced the belief that I was capable of change. Each goal I accomplished, no matter how modest, reminded me that it was never too late to create a life I loved.

Practical Tools for Transformation

The tools that helped me transform my life aren't complicated, but they are powerful when used consistently:

1. **Daily Gratitude Journal**: Every morning, write down three things you're grateful for. This simple practice shifts your focus from scarcity to abundance.
2. **SMART Goals Framework**: Break your goals into specific, measurable, and achievable steps. For example, instead

of saying, *"I want to learn a new skill,"* commit to practicing that skill for 15 minutes a day.

3. **Regular Journaling**: Use a journal to reflect on your thoughts, clarify your goals, and challenge limiting beliefs. Writing things down creates a tangible connection to your aspirations.

These tools aren't magic. They won't transform your life overnight. But if you use them consistently, they will create the foundation for meaningful change.

Looking back, the transformation I experienced didn't happen in one dramatic moment. It happened in the quiet, consistent actions I took each day. It happened in the decision to revisit my dreams, to confront my fears, and to believe in the possibility of a second act.

This journey isn't unique to me. It's available to anyone who's willing to take the first step. And if there's one thing I've learned, it's this: it's never too late to begin again.

CHAPTER 2: BREAKING THE CHAINS OF *"TOO LATE"* THINKING

John, the Doubter

John sat across from me in my office, his shoulders slightly hunched, his hands clasped tightly in his lap. He had the look of someone carrying a weight he couldn't quite put down. At 56, John had spent more than two decades working in a corporate role he described as *"safe."* It paid the bills, kept him comfortable, and provided stability for his family. But comfort doesn't always mean fulfillment, and John's eyes betrayed the weariness of a man who felt trapped by his own choices.

"I just feel like it's too late for me," he said finally, breaking the silence. *"I've been doing this job for so long, and it's not like I'm bad at it. But it's not what I want to do. It never really was."*

The confession seemed to take him by surprise, as if the words had escaped before he had the chance to reel them back in. He shook his head and let out a nervous laugh. *"But who changes careers at 56? I mean, let's be real. That ship has sailed."*

A Safe Life That Felt Empty

John's story was one I'd heard many times before. He'd taken his job in his early thirties, intending it to be a stepping stone to something greater. But as the years passed, stepping stones became foundations. Promotions came, along with a steady paycheck and the kind of predictability that made life manageable.

And yet, John felt anything but fulfilled. He spoke of a lingering dissatisfaction, a sense that he'd spent years building a life that looked good on paper but felt hollow in reality.

"What would you do if you could start over?" I asked him.

John didn't answer right away. Instead, he looked down at his hands, his fingers fidgeting with the edge of his sleeve.

"I've always wanted to teach," he said finally, his voice barely above a whisper. *"I used to think about becoming a history teacher. I even started taking classes once, years ago. But then..."*

He trailed off, shrugging as if the reasons didn't matter anymore. But they did matter, and I pressed him gently.

"What stopped you?"

"Life," he said with a bitter laugh. *"Work. Bills. Kids. And now... now it just feels like it's too late. I don't have the time, the energy, or even the right to change everything now. People are counting on me to keep things steady."*

The Struggle Beneath the Surface

As we talked, it became clear that John's doubts weren't just about practicality. They were rooted in something deeper: fear. Fear of failure. Fear of being judged. Fear of stepping into the unknown after so many years of staying in his comfort zone.

"Everyone expects me to keep doing what I've always done," he said. *"And maybe they're right. Maybe I should just be grateful for what I have and stop chasing things that don't make sense at my age."*

But even as he spoke those words, there was a flicker of something else—a longing he couldn't quite suppress.

"It's not that I don't want to try," he admitted. *"It's that I'm afraid I'll fail. And at my age, failure feels... final."*

The Power of Belief

John's story wasn't unique, but it was deeply personal. He wasn't just battling external challenges; he was wrestling with his own belief system.

Psychologists call this a *self-fulfilling prophecy*. It's the idea that what we believe about ourselves shapes our actions—and ultimately, our outcomes. If John believed it was too late to change, he would act in ways that reinforced that belief. He'd avoid taking risks, dismiss opportunities, and retreat further into the safety of what he knew, even if it didn't fulfill him.

But what if that belief wasn't true?

"What if your age isn't a barrier but an asset?" I asked him.

John looked skeptical, but I could see the question had planted a seed.

"Think about it," I continued. *"You have decades of experience, skills, and wisdom that you didn't have in your twenties. You know how to navigate challenges, how to adapt, how to persevere. What if those things make you more prepared, not less, to pursue something new?"*

Breaking Free from the Chains

Changing John's mindset wasn't going to happen overnight. Years of fear and self-doubt had built walls that wouldn't come down easily. But I could see that he wanted to believe it was possible.

"Let's start small," I suggested. *"What's one thing you can do this week to explore the idea of teaching? It doesn't have to be big. Just a step."*

He thought about it for a moment before nodding. *"I could look into the certification process,"* he said. *"Just see what it would take."*

"That's a great start," I told him. *"And from there, we'll figure out the next step. One step at a time."*

A Window of Possibility

John left that day with a sense of cautious hope. He wasn't ready to overhaul his life, but he was willing to entertain the idea that change was possible. And sometimes, that's all it takes to begin.

In the weeks that followed, John took more steps. He researched certification programs, reached out to a former professor for advice, and even signed up for an online course in education. Each action, no matter how small, chipped away at the belief that it was too late for him to change.

John's story is a reminder that the chains of *"too late"* thinking are often self-imposed. And just as we create those chains, we have the power to break them.

The Science Behind Limiting Beliefs

Imagine standing at the edge of a swimming pool, toes curled over the edge, staring at the water. The surface shimmers invitingly, but your mind whispers all the reasons why you shouldn't jump. *What if the water's too cold? What if you can't swim as well as you used to? What if you sink instead of float?*

For many of us, this is what limiting beliefs feel like. They aren't loud or dramatic; they're quiet whispers that make us hesitate, holding us back from action with a subtle but powerful grip. These whispers are the foundation of cognitive distortions—ways our minds twist reality into something more fearful, more absolute, and far less forgiving.

All-or-Nothing Thinking

One of the most common cognitive distortions is *"all-or-nothing thinking."* It's the belief that if something can't be done perfectly, it shouldn't be done at all. For John, from the previous section, this sounded like, *If I can't start over completely, what's the point of trying at all?*

All-or-nothing thinking creates a false dichotomy: success or failure, perfection or disaster, victory or defeat. It leaves no room for nuance, no space for the messy, imperfect process of growth.

In reality, life is rarely all or nothing. It's a spectrum, a series of incremental steps that lead to progress. But when all-or-nothing thinking takes hold, it convinces us that anything less than perfection is failure, and failure becomes something to avoid at all costs.

The Trap of Catastrophizing

Closely tied to all-or-nothing thinking is *"catastrophizing."* This distortion magnifies challenges, turning them into insurmountable obstacles. It takes a single misstep and imagines the worst possible outcome.

For someone considering a career change, catastrophizing might sound like, *If I try something new and fail, I'll lose everything. People will think I'm foolish. I'll end up with nothing.*

Catastrophizing paralyzes us because it makes the potential risks feel so overwhelming that the rewards seem irrelevant. Instead of focusing on the possibility of growth, we become fixated on avoiding pain.

These distortions aren't just mental habits; they're self-fulfilling prophecies. When we believe failure is inevitable, we act in ways that make failure more likely. We avoid taking risks, we hold back from opportunities, and we reinforce the very beliefs that keep us stuck.

Introducing the Growth Mindset

If limiting beliefs are chains, then a growth mindset is the key that unlocks them. Dr. Carol Dweck, a renowned psychologist, defines the growth mindset as the belief that abilities and intelligence can be developed through effort and persistence.

This mindset stands in direct opposition to the fixed mindset, which sees abilities as static and unchangeable. In a fixed mindset, failure is a reflection of your inherent limitations. In a growth mindset, failure is an opportunity to learn and improve.

When John began to shift toward a growth mindset, he started asking new questions. Instead of, *What if I fail?* he asked, *What can I learn from trying?* Instead of focusing on what he couldn't do yet, he began to explore what he could do now.

The beauty of the growth mindset is that it allows us to see life as a journey, not a destination. It frees us from the pressure of perfection and opens the door to possibility.

The Role of Self-Efficacy

If the growth mindset is the key, then self-efficacy is the engine that drives change. Self-efficacy, a concept developed by psychologist Albert Bandura, refers to our belief in our ability to influence events and outcomes.

Bandura's research shows that when we believe we can achieve something, we're more likely to take the actions necessary to achieve it. This belief isn't about blind optimism; it's about cultivating a realistic confidence in our ability to learn, adapt, and grow.

Think of self-efficacy as the muscle that supports a growth mindset. The more you use it, the stronger it becomes. When John started taking small, deliberate steps toward his goal of teaching, he was building his self-efficacy. Each step reinforced the belief that he could create change, and that belief fueled his willingness to take the next step.

Changing the Narrative

Understanding the science behind limiting beliefs is the first step to overcoming them. When you recognize the cognitive distortions that shape your thinking, you can begin to challenge them.

Ask yourself:

- Am I falling into all-or-nothing thinking?
- Am I catastrophizing potential outcomes?
- Am I allowing a fixed mindset to limit my growth?

Replacing these distortions with a growth mindset and cultivating self-efficacy isn't about ignoring risks or pretending challenges don't exist. It's about seeing those challenges as opportunities rather than barriers.

A Window of Possibility

The science of belief teaches us that change is possible—not because the challenges we face disappear, but because our ability to face them grows. When we choose to believe in our potential, we give ourselves permission to act. And when we act, we discover just how much we're capable of achieving.

Understanding cognitive distortions, embracing a growth mindset, and cultivating self-efficacy are powerful tools for breaking the chains of *"too late"* thinking. They remind us that our stories aren't written in stone and that we have the power to write new chapters, no matter where we are in life.

John's Breakthrough

John sat at his desk, a half-empty cup of coffee next to a notebook filled with scribbled notes and crossed-out ideas. The faint hum of his computer blended with the early morning quiet of his home office. It had been months since our first conversation, and something was different about him.

He wasn't staring blankly into the distance, weighed down by his thoughts. He wasn't trapped in the loop of regret and self-doubt that had defined so much of his life before. Today, John was writing—not just ideas, but a plan. A real, tangible plan to move toward the life he had always dreamed of.

Challenging the Inner Critic

John's journey didn't start with action. It started with a shift in mindset. Like many of us, he had spent years listening to his inner critic—a relentless voice that reminded him of every mistake, every missed opportunity, every reason why change wasn't possible.

"I used to tell myself it was too late," he admitted during one of our sessions. *"Too late to start over. Too late to do something meaningful. But then I realized... that voice isn't the truth. It's just a story I've been telling myself."*

Together, we worked on identifying and challenging that inner voice. One of the first tools I introduced him to was a *thought journal.* Each time he caught himself thinking, *I'm too old for this,* or, *I'll never succeed,* he wrote it down. Then, he asked himself three questions:

1. Is this thought absolutely true?
2. What evidence supports this thought?
3. What evidence contradicts it?

At first, the exercise felt uncomfortable. John was used to taking his thoughts at face value. But as he wrote, he began to see patterns in his thinking—patterns rooted in fear, not fact.

One day, he shared an entry from his journal.

Thought: *I'm too old to start a new career.*

Evidence: *I've been in my current job for 20 years, and I haven't done anything new in a long time.*

Contradicting Evidence: *I've learned new skills throughout my career. I'm a quick learner. I know how to adapt.*

"That last part surprised me," John said. *"I didn't realize how much I've actually accomplished over the years. I've been so focused on what I haven't done that I forgot all the ways I've grown."*

Taking the First Steps

Once John began to reframe his limiting beliefs, he was ready to take action. But instead of jumping headfirst into a complete career overhaul, he started small.

"I knew I couldn't change everything overnight," he said. *"So I focused on what I could do right now."*

One of his first steps was to reach out to a friend who worked in education—an industry he'd always been curious about. They met for coffee, and John asked questions about what it was like to teach, what challenges came with the job, and how someone like him might transition into the field.

"That conversation was a game-changer," he told me. *"It made me realize that the barriers I'd built up in my head weren't as big as I thought. I just needed to take it one step at a time."*

John also began volunteering at a local community center, teaching basic computer skills to adults. It wasn't his dream job, but it was a step in the right direction. And each time he walked into that classroom, he felt a little more confident in his ability to make a difference.

Building a Support System

One of the most powerful tools in John's journey was his support system. Change is hard, and trying to do it alone can make it feel impossible.

John started by sharing his goals with his family. At first, he was hesitant. *"What if they think I'm crazy?"* he wondered. But their response surprised him.

"They were excited," he said, his voice tinged with emotion. *"They told me they were proud of me for wanting to pursue something meaningful. That gave me the courage to keep going."*

In addition to his family, John joined a local professional group for career changers. Meeting others who were navigating similar challenges reminded him that he wasn't alone. Their stories inspired him, and their encouragement kept him moving forward on days when doubt crept back in.

Using Affirmations and Visualization

Another tool John embraced was affirmations. At first, he thought they sounded cheesy—*"like something out of a self-*

help book," he joked. But as he started using them, he noticed a shift in his mindset.

Every morning, John stood in front of his bathroom mirror and repeated three simple affirmations:

1. I am capable of change.
2. I am worthy of pursuing my dreams.
3. I am taking steps toward a meaningful life.

"I felt silly at first," he admitted. *"But over time, those words started to feel real. They became part of how I saw myself."*

He also began using visualization to imagine his future. Before bed each night, he closed his eyes and pictured himself teaching a classroom full of engaged students. He imagined the conversations, the connections, the sense of purpose he would feel.

"These exercises helped me see what was possible," he said. *"And once I could see it, I started to believe it."*

The Power of Momentum

One of the most important lessons John learned was the power of momentum. Change didn't come from one big leap; it came from a series of small, consistent actions.

Each week, he created a simple action plan. It included three things he could do to move closer to his goal, no matter how small. One week, it was researching certification programs.

Another week, it was applying for a part-time teaching assistant position.

"With every step, I felt like I was proving something to myself," John said. *"Not just that I could do it, but that I was becoming the kind of person who takes action."*

The Transformation

Six months after John first came to me, he stood in front of his first class as a certified teacher. It wasn't the biggest class, and it wasn't the most glamorous job, but it was a start.

"I never thought I'd be here," he said, his voice filled with gratitude. *"But now that I am, I can't imagine doing anything else."*

John's journey wasn't about achieving perfection. It was about proving to himself that it's never too late to change. By challenging his inner critic, taking small steps, and leaning on his support system, he created a life that aligned with his passions and values.

Practical Tools for Transformation

Here are the tools that helped John create his breakthrough:

1. **Thought Journal**: Write down limiting beliefs as they arise. Challenge them by asking if they're true and identifying evidence that contradicts them.

2. **Weekly Action Plan**: Set three achievable goals each week to build momentum. Focus on progress, not perfection.
3. **Affirmations and Visualization**: Use positive affirmations to shift your mindset, and visualize your desired future to keep your goals in focus.
4. **Support System**: Share your journey with trusted friends, family, or professional groups. Their encouragement can make all the difference.

John's story is proof that the chains of *"too late"* thinking can be broken. And once they are, the possibilities are endless.

Chapter 3: Rediscovering Your Forgotten Dreams

My Journey Back to Woodworking

The workshop smelled of sawdust and varnish, a scent I hadn't inhaled in years. The tools lay scattered on the workbench like forgotten memories, each one carrying the weight of a story I hadn't told in decades. My hand hovered over an old chisel, its wooden handle worn smooth from years of use—back when this workshop wasn't just a room but a sanctuary.

It had been over twenty years since I'd picked up a piece of wood and thought about turning it into something beautiful. Life, as it often does, had gotten in the way. Careers, kids, bills—all the responsibilities that come with adulthood had quietly edged out the passions that once filled my days.

But here I was, standing in the space that had once felt like a second home, wondering if I could still remember how to create.

Letting Go of Forgotten Passions

Woodworking had been more than a hobby to me—it was a way to lose myself in the rhythm of creating something tangible. I loved the feel of the grain beneath my fingertips, the satisfying rasp of the plane smoothing out imperfections, the slow transformation of raw wood into something with purpose and beauty.

But as the demands of life increased, I began to tell myself that there wasn't room for indulgences like this. There were always more pressing things to do: work deadlines, soccer games, endless to-do lists. Little by little, I stopped coming out to the workshop. The tools gathered dust, and the woodpile in the corner shrank to nothing.

At first, I told myself it was temporary. *"I'll get back to it when things settle down,"* I thought. But the years passed, and *"when things settle down"* never came.

The Emotional Barriers

Returning to the workshop after so many years wasn't easy. It felt like confronting a version of myself I'd left behind—a younger, more optimistic version who believed there was always time to pursue the things that brought joy.

I was flooded with mixed emotions. There was guilt, for one. How could I justify spending time on something that was *"just for me"* when there were so many other demands on my time? There was also fear. What if I'd lost whatever skill I once had? What if I failed? And then there was the belief that had taken root in my mind over the years: *Dreams are for the young. At my age, it's too late to pick up something like this.*

Those thoughts weighed heavily on me as I stood in that workshop. But they weren't the only thing I felt. There was also a spark of something else—something I hadn't felt in years. It was curiosity. Excitement. A quiet voice whispering, *What if you can still do this?*

A Shaky Start

The first time I tried to make something again, it didn't go well. My hands felt clumsy, as if they belonged to someone else. The measurements were off, the cuts uneven. The piece of wood I'd chosen—a simple block of oak—refused to cooperate.

I felt frustration creeping in, along with the familiar temptation to give up. *"What's the point?"* I thought. *"You're not good at this anymore."*

But then I caught myself. I thought about all the times I'd told myself that same story in other areas of my life—times when I'd let fear or frustration stop me from pursuing something meaningful.

"This isn't about being good at it," I reminded myself. *"It's about doing it."*

So I kept going. I made mistakes. I ruined a few pieces of wood. But with each attempt, I felt a little more at home in the process. I started to remember the rhythms of the work, the joy of seeing something take shape under my hands.

Why Hobbies Matter

What I didn't fully understand at the time was how important this rediscovery was for my sense of identity. Psychologists have long studied the role of hobbies and personal interests in maintaining mental and emotional well-being. These activities aren't just distractions; they're a way to connect with who we are outside of our roles and responsibilities.

When we abandon the things that bring us joy, we risk losing touch with ourselves. We become defined solely by what we do for others—our careers, our families, our obligations. But hobbies remind us that we are more than the sum of our responsibilities. They give us a sense of autonomy, creativity, and fulfillment.

Returning to woodworking wasn't just about making furniture. It was about reclaiming a part of myself I thought I'd lost.

A New Perspective

As the weeks went by, my confidence grew. I finished my first project—a simple stool—and while it wasn't perfect, it was mine. I stood back and looked at it, feeling a sense of accomplishment I hadn't felt in years.

It wasn't just the stool that mattered. It was what it represented: a step toward reconnecting with a passion I'd allowed to fade. It reminded me that it's never too late to pick up something you love, to rediscover the things that make you feel alive.

And as I spent more time in the workshop, I noticed something unexpected: the lessons I was learning there were spilling over into other areas of my life. I was more patient, more willing to take risks, more open to the idea that growth is a lifelong process.

The Emotional Rewards

One evening, as I was sanding the edge of a table I'd been working on, my youngest son wandered into the workshop. He watched me for a while before asking, *"What are you making?"*

"A table," I said, smiling.

"Can I help?"

In that moment, I realized something profound. By reconnecting with my own passions, I wasn't just doing something for myself—I was modeling for my children the importance of pursuing what you love.

That evening, as we worked together on the table, I felt an overwhelming sense of gratitude. For the first time in years, I wasn't just existing. I was living.

The Invitation

My journey back to woodworking taught me that it's never too late to rediscover the things that bring you joy. Those passions, no matter how long you've ignored them, are still there, waiting for you. And when you make space for them, you open the door to a fuller, more meaningful life.

If there's a dream or hobby you've set aside, I encourage you to revisit it. Start small. Let go of the need to be perfect. Focus on the process, not the outcome.

You might be surprised by what you find—and by the person you become in the process.

Why Dreams Matter for Fulfillment

The question lingered in the back of my mind for years: *Why did I let this go?* It wasn't just about woodworking or any specific passion. It was the realization that I had set aside pieces of myself, pieces that once made me feel alive, in favor of obligations, responsibilities, and the steady drumbeat of daily life.

As I began to reconnect with my dreams, I discovered something deeper: our dreams aren't just hobbies or distractions. They're intimately tied to who we are, what we value, and how we find meaning in life. They're not luxuries—they're necessities.

Dreams as a Compass

Have you ever noticed how certain activities or aspirations make you feel more like yourself? Maybe it's painting, playing an instrument, writing, or traveling. These aren't random interests—they're reflections of your core values and identity.

Dreams act as a compass, guiding us toward what truly matters. When we pursue them, we align ourselves with our values—whether those values are creativity, connection, adventure, or growth. But when we ignore or suppress our dreams, we risk losing touch with those values, leaving us feeling unfulfilled and adrift.

I realized this during one of my first sessions back in the workshop. As I shaped a block of wood into something purposeful, I wasn't just engaging in a long-forgotten hobby. I was reconnecting with a part of myself that valued craftsmanship, patience, and the joy of creation. It wasn't about the finished product—it was about who I became in the process.

For years, I had ignored that compass. I had let the demands of life steer me away from the things that once gave me direction and meaning. But here's what I learned: those dreams never truly disappear. They wait patiently for us to rediscover them.

The Six Human Needs

Tony Robbins often speaks about the six human needs that drive our behavior: certainty, variety, significance, connection, growth, and contribution. These needs are universal, but the ways we fulfill them are deeply personal. And for many of us, our dreams hold the key to meeting some of these needs in profound and fulfilling ways.

Take growth, for example. When we pursue a dream—whether it's learning a new skill, starting a business, or traveling to a new place—we stretch ourselves. We step out of our comfort zones, embrace challenges, and discover what we're capable of. Growth is an essential part of feeling alive, and dreams give us the opportunity to experience it.

Then there's contribution. Our dreams aren't just about personal fulfillment; they often involve making a difference in the lives of others. Whether it's sharing your art, teaching a skill, or building something that benefits your community, pursuing your passions allows you to contribute to the world in meaningful ways.

When I returned to woodworking, I initially thought it was just for me. But as I began sharing my creations with family and friends, I saw how much joy it brought them. My youngest son, inspired by my renewed enthusiasm, started spending time with me in the workshop. What began as a personal journey became an opportunity to connect and contribute to the people I love most.

Visualization: Reigniting the Spark

One of the most powerful tools I used to reconnect with my dreams was visualization. At first, it felt silly—like daydreaming with a purpose. But the more I practiced it, the more I realized its potential.

Visualization isn't just imagining what you want to achieve; it's about immersing yourself in the experience of your dream. Research on mental imagery shows that when we vividly imagine ourselves achieving a goal, our brain responds as if we're actually doing it. This process not only boosts motivation but also helps us overcome the mental barriers that hold us back.

I began visualizing myself back in the workshop, not just building furniture but feeling the satisfaction of creating something with my own hands. I pictured the sawdust settling on the floor, the rhythmic hum of the tools, and the pride of standing back to admire a finished piece.

These mental images weren't just fantasies—they were fuel. They reminded me why I loved woodworking in the first place and gave me the confidence to pick up my tools again.

Why Dreams Matter

As I reflected on my journey, one truth became clear: dreams aren't just about achieving something tangible. They're about the person you become in the pursuit of them.

Pursuing a dream teaches you resilience, patience, and the value of imperfection. It connects you with your values and reminds you of your capacity for growth and contribution. Most importantly, it reignites a sense of purpose—a reminder that life is meant to be lived fully, not just endured.

The beauty of rediscovering your dreams is that it doesn't require a perfect plan or unlimited resources. It starts with a willingness to listen to that quiet voice inside you, the one that whispers, *What if?*

What if you picked up that paintbrush again? What if you dusted off that guitar? What if you allowed yourself to imagine a life where your passions took center stage?

A Path Forward

The path to rediscovering your dreams isn't always easy, but it's always worth it. It requires letting go of the belief that dreams are impractical or indulgent and embracing the idea that they are vital to your fulfillment.

Here's how you can start:

1. **Identify Your Compass**: Reflect on the activities or aspirations that once made you feel alive. What did you love to do as a child or young adult? What passions have you set aside?

2. **Visualize the Possibility**: Spend a few minutes each day imagining yourself pursuing your dream. Focus on the emotions, sensations, and satisfaction it brings.

3. **Take One Small Step**: Dreams don't come to life overnight. Start with a single action—buy a sketchbook, sign up for a class, or set aside 30 minutes to reconnect with your passion.

Rediscovering your forgotten dreams isn't about reclaiming lost time. It's about embracing the time you have now to live with intention and joy. Dreams are more than aspirations—they're a bridge to a life that feels true to who you are.

And no matter where you are in life, it's never too late to cross that bridge.

My Renewed Passion and Success

The soft hum of the sander echoed through the workshop, blending with the gentle rustling of leaves outside. The scent of freshly cut wood filled the air, mingling with the faint tang of varnish. I stood at my workbench, running my hands over a smooth, finished tabletop. It had been weeks of careful planning, precise cuts, and a few mistakes along the way, but here it was—a tangible reminder that some things, no matter how long forgotten, are never truly lost.

Bringing woodworking back into my life wasn't just about making furniture. It was about rediscovering a part of myself I thought I'd left behind. It started small—tentative steps that grew into something transformative.

The Power of Visualization

One of the most effective tools I used to rekindle my passion was visualization. At first, it felt strange, even a little indulgent, to spend time imagining myself working in the workshop again. But the more I practiced, the more real it became.

Each morning, I sat quietly for a few minutes, closing my eyes and picturing the process. I imagined the feel of the wood grain under my hands, the satisfying weight of the tools, and the sound of the saw cutting cleanly through the plank. I pictured the finished product—something sturdy, beautiful, and uniquely mine.

Visualization didn't just motivate me; it helped me overcome the fear and inertia that had kept me away for so long. It reminded me of the joy I felt in the process, even when things didn't go perfectly.

Research supports this practice. Studies on mental imagery show that imagining yourself successfully engaging in an activity activates the same neural pathways as actually doing it. Visualization becomes a mental rehearsal, building confidence and reducing anxiety about taking action.

Making Time for What Matters

Of course, visualization alone wasn't enough. I had to carve out actual time in my schedule—time that felt scarce amid work, family obligations, and the endless list of daily responsibilities.

I started small, setting aside just 30 minutes twice a week to spend in the workshop. At first, it felt like an indulgence, but I quickly realized it was an investment in my well-being.

To make it work, I treated those sessions as non-negotiable appointments. They were written into my calendar, just like meetings or errands. And just like those commitments, I showed up—even when I didn't feel like it.

Something interesting happened as I kept showing up: the more time I spent reconnecting with woodworking, the more energized I felt in other areas of my life. Those 30-

minute sessions expanded as I realized how much joy and fulfillment they brought me. What started as a small commitment grew into a central part of my routine.

Inspiring Others

What surprised me most about this journey wasn't just how much it enriched my own life—it was how it inspired the people around me.

One evening, my wife walked into the workshop, watching as I carefully assembled the legs of a new chair. *"You seem different lately,"* she said, her voice warm. *"Happier. Lighter."*

I looked up, realizing she was right. *"I think I am,"* I said.

She smiled. *"It's nice to see you doing this again."*

Her encouragement meant the world to me. It made me realize that when we pursue our passions, it doesn't just benefit us—it radiates outward, affecting the people we care about most.

Even my clients began to notice the change. As I shared my story with them—how I had rediscovered something I loved and made it a priority in my life—they began to reflect on their own dreams.

One client, inspired by my journey, decided to pick up his guitar again after more than a decade. Another began writing short stories, something she'd always loved but never made time for.

"It's funny," one of them said during a session. *"I thought dreams were supposed to be selfish, but they're not, are they? They make us better, for ourselves and everyone around us."*

The Ripple Effect

The ripple effect of reconnecting with my passion extended beyond my family and clients. It changed the way I approached challenges, both personal and professional. I became more patient, more willing to embrace imperfection, and more open to taking risks.

Woodworking taught me lessons I hadn't expected—about persistence, creativity, and the value of starting over when things don't go as planned. Those lessons spilled over into my work and relationships, helping me navigate life with greater confidence and resilience.

Most importantly, it reminded me that it's never too late to reclaim the things that make you feel alive.

Actionable Steps to Reconnect with Your Passion

If you're ready to rediscover a forgotten dream or passion, here are a few tools that worked for me:

1. **Create a Dream Journal**: Start by writing down the passions or hobbies you've set aside. Reflect on why they mattered to you and how they made you feel. This process helps you reconnect with your motivations and values.

2. **Visualize Success**: Spend a few minutes each day imagining yourself engaging in your passion. Focus on the sensory details—what you see, hear, feel, and experience. This practice helps build confidence and motivation.

3. **Set a Realistic Plan**: Begin with small, manageable steps. Block out time in your schedule, even if it's just 15 minutes a week, to reconnect with your passion. Treat it as a priority, not an afterthought.

4. **Share Your Journey**: Talk to your loved ones about your dream. Their encouragement and support can make a huge difference, and sharing your story might even inspire them to pursue their own passions.

The Gift of Renewal

Looking back, I'm struck by how much this journey has given me—not just in terms of what I've created, but in how I see myself and my life. Reconnecting with woodworking didn't just bring joy and fulfillment; it reminded me of what's possible when we make space for the things we love.

And that's the gift I hope to share with you: the realization that it's never too late to reignite your passion, to rediscover the dreams you thought you'd lost, and to create a life that feels authentically yours.

Part 2:

Build the Life You've Always Wanted

CHAPTER 4:

HEALTH, ENERGY, AND VITALITY - STARTING NOW

My Midlife Health Wake-Up

The moment of truth came on a random Tuesday morning. I was standing in front of the mirror, struggling to button a shirt I hadn't worn in months. It wasn't just the tightness of the fabric or the extra weight around my midsection that caught my attention—it was the man staring back at me. He looked tired. His posture was slumped, his energy drained. He looked like someone who had been running on empty for far too long.

I took a deep breath and let it out slowly. *"How did I let it get this far?"* I asked myself.

A Slow Drift into Neglect

The truth is, it hadn't happened overnight. Like so many men in midlife, I had spent years focused on everything but my own health. My career was demanding, my family needed me, and there were always a dozen reasons to put off taking care of myself.

It started with little things—skipping workouts because I was too busy, grabbing fast food because it was convenient, staying up late to finish work instead of getting a full night's sleep. Those little things added up.

By the time I turned 50, the signs were impossible to ignore. I felt sluggish almost every day. My weight had crept up steadily, and I didn't have the energy to keep up with my kids, let alone pursue the hobbies I loved. Even walking up a flight of stairs left me winded.

It wasn't just the physical symptoms that bothered me. There was a deeper sense of dissatisfaction—a feeling that I wasn't living up to the person I wanted to be.

Facing the Mirror

That morning in front of the mirror wasn't the first time I'd noticed the changes, but it was the first time I couldn't look away. I had always told myself I'd get back on track *"someday."* But as I stood there, struggling to button that shirt, I realized someday wasn't coming. If I didn't make a change now, I might never make one.

The thought terrified me. I didn't want to become the kind of man who let his best years slip away because he was too afraid or too overwhelmed to take action.

Overwhelmed and Unsure

The biggest challenge wasn't acknowledging that I needed to change—it was figuring out where to start. The advice out there was overwhelming: diets, workout plans, supplements, and endless *"hacks"* promising quick results.

It felt like there were a thousand steps I needed to take, and I didn't know which one to take first. The overwhelm was paralyzing, and for a while, it kept me stuck in the same cycle of inaction.

I remember sitting at the kitchen table one evening, scrolling through articles about weight loss and fitness. The more I read, the more hopeless I felt. Every plan seemed too extreme, too complicated, or too focused on things I didn't care about.

"What's the point?" I muttered under my breath. *"It's too late anyway."*

But deep down, I knew that wasn't true. I knew that if I kept making excuses, I'd only feel worse.

The Wake-Up Call

What finally pushed me to act wasn't a dramatic event. It was a small, quiet moment with my son.

One Saturday afternoon, he asked me to play soccer with him in the backyard. I wanted to say yes—I really did—but I hesitated. I was tired, my knees ached, and the thought of running around for even a few minutes felt daunting.

I saw the disappointment in his eyes when I told him, *"Maybe later."* And in that moment, I realized I was letting my health—or lack of it—limit the kind of father I wanted to be.

That was my wake-up call. I didn't want to miss out on moments like that because I hadn't taken care of myself.

The Effects of Aging and Inactivity

As I began researching how to improve my health, I came across startling statistics about the effects of aging and inactivity. Studies show that after the age of 30, men lose muscle mass and strength at a rate of about 3-5% per decade if they remain inactive. This decline doesn't just affect physical strength—it impacts metabolism, energy levels, and overall quality of life.

Inactivity also has profound effects on mental health. Research highlights the connection between sedentary lifestyles and increased rates of depression, anxiety, and cognitive decline. It was a sobering reminder that neglecting my health wasn't just a physical issue—it was a mental and emotional one as well.

I didn't want to become a statistic. I wanted to reclaim my energy, my confidence, and my sense of vitality.

Relatable Struggles

Looking back, I know my story isn't unique. Many men reach a point in their lives where they realize they've been putting their health on the back burner for far too long. The weight gain, the low energy, the feeling of being stuck—it's something so many of us experience.

But here's what I want you to know: it's never too late to make a change. No matter how far you feel you've drifted, you can start steering your life in a new direction.

That moment in the mirror, that quiet wake-up call from my son, became the catalyst for change. I didn't have all the answers, and I didn't know exactly how to get where I wanted to go. But I knew I had to start.

In the chapters ahead, we'll explore practical, sustainable ways to rebuild your health and energy. You don't need a perfect plan or a complete overhaul. All you need is the willingness to take the first step.

And that first step? It starts today.

Rewiring Your Mindset About Health

I still remember the day I realized that making a change wasn't about overhauling my entire life—it was about starting small. I had been trying to motivate myself for weeks, telling myself that I needed to go to the gym five days a week or cut out every indulgence from my diet. But every time I set those lofty goals, I'd fall short and feel worse about myself.

Then I came across a simple concept that changed everything: the idea of compounding habits.

The Power of Small, Consistent Actions

The first time I read about compounding habits, it was like a light bulb went off in my mind. The idea, popularized by James Clear in *Atomic Habits*, is deceptively simple: small, consistent actions add up to massive results over time. It's the same principle that makes a tiny snowball rolling down a hill grow into a boulder.

I decided to test it for myself. Instead of committing to an hour-long workout, I started with five minutes of stretching every morning. Instead of trying to overhaul my diet, I focused on drinking one extra glass of water each day. These changes felt almost laughably small, but that was the point—they were too easy to fail.

At first, I didn't notice much of a difference. But as the days turned into weeks, those small actions began to build momentum. Five minutes of stretching turned into ten, then twenty. One glass of water became two, then three. Each small victory gave me the confidence to take the next step.

What I realized was that the hardest part of change isn't the action itself—it's starting. Once you take that first step, the second step feels a little easier. And before you know it, those steps become a path.

The effectiveness of compounding habits is rooted in psychology and neuroscience. Our brains thrive on patterns, and when we repeat an action consistently, it becomes automatic—a habit.

Consider this: when you first learn to drive, every movement feels deliberate and effortful. You think about every turn of the wheel, every press of the pedal. But over time, those actions become second nature. Habits work the same way.

Small actions might not feel significant in the moment, but they create neural pathways that strengthen with repetition. Over time, those pathways become the foundation for lasting change.

State Management: Fueling Energy and Motivation

Once I started building momentum with small habits, I began to notice a subtle but powerful shift in how I felt. My energy levels improved, my mood lifted, and I found it easier to stay motivated. That's when I discovered Tony Robbins' concept of state management.

State management is the idea that your physical state—how you move, what you eat, and what you focus on—has a direct impact on your energy and motivation. It's not just about what you do; it's about how you feel while you're doing it.

Tony often says, *"Motion creates emotion."* And he's right. When you're feeling sluggish or unmotivated, the quickest way to change your state is to move.

I started incorporating small bursts of movement into my day—stretching, a quick walk around the block, or even just standing up and doing a few jumping jacks. These actions took less than five minutes, but they had an immediate effect on my mood and energy.

The science backs this up. Physical movement triggers the release of endorphins—chemicals in the brain that act as natural mood elevators. Exercise also increases levels of serotonin, which helps regulate mood and improve cognitive function.

The more I moved, the better I felt. And the better I felt, the more motivated I was to keep going.

I also began paying attention to how my diet affected my energy. Instead of focusing on what I couldn't eat, I started adding more of what my body needed: whole foods, plenty of water, and the occasional green smoothie.

Tony's teachings emphasize that food is fuel. The quality of what you put into your body determines the quality of energy you get out of it. This simple shift in mindset—from restriction to nourishment—helped me make better choices without feeling deprived.

The final piece of state management is focus. What you choose to focus on determines how you feel and what you do. When I focused on how far I had to go or how much I needed to change, I felt overwhelmed. But when I focused on the small wins—the extra glass of water, the five minutes of movement—I felt encouraged.

Tony calls this *"priming,"* the practice of intentionally directing your focus to what's positive and empowering. Each morning, I spent a few minutes reflecting on what I was grateful for and what I wanted to accomplish that day. This simple exercise helped set the tone for everything that followed.

Rewiring My Relationship with Health

As I began to embrace these principles—compounding habits, state management, and intentional focus—I noticed something profound: I no longer saw health as a daunting goal. It became a journey, one I looked forward to rather than dreaded.

The small actions I took each day weren't just about improving my physical health. They were about creating a sense of control and confidence in my life. They reminded me that even the smallest steps could lead to meaningful change.

Actionable Steps to Rewire Your Mindset

If you're ready to rewrite your relationship with health, here are a few practical steps to get started:

1. **Start Small**: Choose one simple action you can commit to today, whether it's drinking an extra glass of water, taking a short walk, or stretching for five minutes.
2. **Focus on Progress, Not Perfection**: Remember, it's not about doing everything at once. It's about building momentum through small, consistent actions.
3. **Move to Shift Your Mood**: When you're feeling stuck or unmotivated, try a quick burst of movement to re-energize yourself.
4. **Fuel Your Body, Not Just Your Goals**: Shift your mindset around food from restriction to nourishment. Focus on adding more of what fuels you rather than cutting things out.

5. **Prime Your Focus**: Start each day by reflecting on what you're grateful for and what you want to achieve. Set an empowering tone for your actions.

A New Perspective

Rewiring your mindset about health isn't about drastic changes or impossible goals. It's about understanding that small, consistent actions can have a profound impact on how you feel, think, and live.

Each step you take—no matter how small—is a step toward a healthier, more energized version of yourself. And that version of you is closer than you think.

My Road to Transformation

The first day was the hardest.

I laced up an old pair of sneakers, glanced at the clock, and stepped outside for what I had decided would be a ten-minute walk. The air was crisp, carrying the faint scent of grass and autumn leaves, but I barely noticed it. My mind was preoccupied with doubts: *Is this even worth it? Ten minutes? What's the point?*

But I pushed those thoughts aside and started walking.

Taking the First Step

That initial walk wasn't about burning calories or setting records. It was about proving something to myself: that I could start. For so long, I'd let inertia hold me back, telling myself that if I couldn't commit to an hour-long workout or an intensive fitness plan, it wasn't worth trying.

But this time, I let go of those expectations. I told myself, *Ten minutes is enough for today.* And it was.

That walk marked the beginning of my transformation—not because it was impressive, but because it was consistent. The next day, I did another ten minutes. Then fifteen. Soon, it became a habit, one that I actually started to enjoy.

As walking became a part of my routine, I started making other small changes. I bought a water bottle and kept it on my desk, reminding myself to drink more water throughout the day. At first, it felt like a chore, but I quickly noticed the difference it made. I felt less tired, more alert, and even my skin looked healthier.

Next, I added two short strength-training sessions to my week. I didn't join a gym or invest in fancy equipment—I used a pair of dumbbells I found in the garage. At first, I kept the workouts simple: squats, push-ups, and a few basic exercises for my arms and core.

These sessions weren't about perfection; they were about progress. I didn't push myself to exhaustion or compare my efforts to anyone else. Instead, I focused on showing up consistently.

Seeing the Changes

The changes didn't happen overnight, but they happened.

Within a few weeks, I noticed that climbing the stairs didn't leave me winded anymore. My clothes started to fit better. I had more energy to play with my kids, to focus at work, and to enjoy the activities I loved.

Even more surprising was the effect on my confidence. As my body grew stronger, so did my belief in my ability to make meaningful changes in other areas of my life.

One morning, I caught my reflection in the mirror and felt something I hadn't felt in a long time: pride.

The Ripple Effect

The benefits of these changes went far beyond physical health. As I built healthier habits, I found myself approaching other aspects of life with the same mindset.

I started setting goals for my career, tackling projects I'd been procrastinating on for years. I reconnected with old friends, reaching out for coffee or a quick phone call. Even my relationships with my family deepened, as I had more energy and patience to truly be present with them.

Each step I took toward better health became a step toward a better version of myself.

Practical Tools for Transformation

Here are some of the tools that helped me along the way:

1. **Habit Trackers**: I used a simple habit tracker to record my daily walks, hydration, and workouts. Seeing those checkmarks add up was incredibly motivating, reminding me that consistency matters more than perfection.
2. **Meal-Planning Framework**: Instead of following a restrictive diet, I adopted a simple meal-planning framework. Each meal included a source of protein, a serving of vegetables, and a healthy carb. This approach kept things flexible and sustainable.
3. **Breathing Techniques for Stress**: Stress had always been a trigger for unhealthy choices, so I started practicing deep breathing techniques during moments of overwhelm. Just five minutes of focused breathing helped me reset and make better decisions.

One Step at a Time

My journey wasn't about dramatic changes or quick fixes. It was about taking one small step at a time, building habits that felt manageable and meaningful.

Each walk, each glass of water, each workout was a choice to prioritize my health—not just for the sake of my body, but for the life I wanted to live.

If there's one thing I've learned, it's this: transformation isn't about how you start. It's about how you keep going.

And the best time to start? It's right now.

CHAPTER 5: THE SECRETS TO REKINDLING PASSION IN LOVE

Paul and Sarah's Struggle for Connection

Paul sat across from me, his shoulders slouched, his hands clasped tightly in his lap. His words came slowly, as though each one was a reluctant visitor. *"I don't know how we got here,"* he said, his voice tinged with frustration and sadness.

He was 58 years old, married to Sarah for nearly three decades. Together, they had built a life filled with shared memories—raising two children, navigating careers, and weathering life's inevitable ups and downs. But now, sitting in my office, Paul admitted that something essential had slipped away.

A Relationship on Autopilot

"It feels like we're just roommates," Paul said. *"We go through the motions—work, dinner, TV, bed. But there's no connection anymore. No passion. I don't even know if she likes me, let alone loves me."*

I nodded, sensing the weight of his words. *"Have you talked to Sarah about how you feel?"*

Paul hesitated, then shook his head. *"I've tried, but it always ends in a fight. She says I don't listen, that I'm too focused on myself. And maybe she's right. But I feel like she doesn't see me anymore—like I'm invisible in my own marriage."*

This is where so many couples find themselves after years of shared routines and unspoken needs. It's not that the love disappears—it's that it gets buried under the weight of daily life, unacknowledged feelings, and unmet expectations.

Sarah's Perspective

A week later, I met with Sarah. She spoke with a mixture of sadness and exasperation, her words revealing the other side of the story.

"I feel like I've been shouting into a void for years," she said. *"I tell him how I feel, what I need, but it's like he doesn't hear me. He just shuts down, and then we're stuck in this cycle of avoidance and frustration."*

She sighed, looking down at her hands. *"It's not that I don't love him—I do. But I feel so... alone. Like I'm carrying the weight of our relationship by myself."*

Her words mirrored Paul's in a way neither of them seemed to realize. Both felt unseen, unheard, and unappreciated. But instead of bringing them together, their shared pain had become a wedge driving them further apart.

The Silent Drift

Paul and Sarah's story is far from unique. Long-term relationships often face this silent drift, where partners grow apart not out of malice, but out of neglect—not of each other, but of the relationship itself.

As routines take over and life's demands pile up, it's easy to put connection on autopilot. Conversations become logistical rather than meaningful. Physical intimacy dwindles. Small gestures of appreciation are replaced by a sense of expectation.

Over time, these patterns erode the emotional foundation of a relationship, leaving both partners feeling isolated, resentful, and unsure of how to find their way back to each other.

The Challenge of Unspoken Needs

One of the biggest hurdles Paul and Sarah faced was the gap between what they needed and what they expressed. Paul longed for appreciation and physical intimacy but struggled to articulate those desires. Sarah craved emotional connection and understanding but felt her attempts to communicate were dismissed or misunderstood.

This is a common dynamic in relationships. We expect our partners to know what we need without having to say it, believing that love should make those needs obvious. But love doesn't grant the ability to read minds. Without open, honest communication, even the strongest relationships can falter.

The Broader Challenge

Paul and Sarah's struggles reflect a universal truth about long-term relationships: maintaining intimacy requires effort. It's not enough to rely on the love that brought you together in the first place. Relationships are living things, and like anything living, they need care and attention to thrive.

Research by Dr. John Gottman, a leading relationship expert, highlights the importance of small, daily gestures in maintaining connection. He refers to these as *"bids for connection"*—moments when one partner reaches out for attention, affection, or support. Whether it's a question, a touch, or a shared laugh, these bids are opportunities to strengthen the bond between partners.

But when those bids are ignored or dismissed, resentment builds. Over time, it creates a cycle of disengagement, where both partners stop reaching out, convinced the other doesn't care.

This is where Paul and Sarah found themselves—stuck in a pattern of unspoken needs and unmet bids for connection.

Hope in the Struggle

Despite the pain and frustration, there was hope for Paul and Sarah, as there is for any couple willing to confront these challenges together. The first step was helping them see that their struggles weren't a sign of failure, but an opportunity for growth.

"Your love is still there," I told them. *"It's just been buried under years of habits and misunderstandings. But if you're willing to dig, you can uncover it again."*

They didn't need to reinvent their relationship overnight. They just needed to take the first step—a willingness to listen, to communicate, and to prioritize connection in a way they hadn't before.

The Invitation

Paul and Sarah's journey wasn't easy, and it didn't resolve itself in a single conversation. But it started with a choice: the choice to fight for their relationship, not against each other.

In the chapters ahead, we'll explore the practical tools and strategies that helped them—and that can help you—reignite passion, deepen emotional connection, and rediscover the joy of love.

Because no matter how far apart you feel, the path back to each other is always within reach.

Understanding the Dynamics of Passion

The soft glow of the evening lamp filled Paul and Sarah's living room as they sat together, attempting to bridge the emotional canyon that had grown between them. Their words were careful, tentative, as though testing the weight of the fragile trust they were trying to rebuild. *"I miss us,"* Sarah finally said, her voice trembling with vulnerability. Paul looked at her, his eyes softening. *"I miss us too,"* he replied. It was a small moment, but one that held the seeds of something transformative: the decision to reconnect.

Vulnerability and Trust: The Foundation of Intimacy

Intimacy—both emotional and physical—thrives on vulnerability. It's the willingness to be seen fully, flaws and all, and to trust that your partner will hold that vulnerability with care. But vulnerability isn't easy, especially in relationships where hurt or resentment has built walls between partners.

Dr. John Gottman's *"Sound Relationship House"* model offers a framework for rebuilding intimacy and trust. At its core are two principles: *turning toward each other* and *creating shared meaning.*

1. **Turning Toward Each Other**: Gottman's research shows that intimacy is built in the small, everyday moments of connection—what he calls *"bids."* These are the subtle requests for attention, affection, or support, like sharing a story about your day or reaching for your partner's hand. When these bids are met with acknowledgment and engagement, trust grows.
2. **Creating Shared Meaning**: This involves developing rituals, goals, and values that both partners hold dear. It's not just about sharing a life but creating a life together that feels meaningful and aligned.

When Paul and Sarah began addressing their struggles, they started small. They committed to a simple practice: acknowledging and responding to each other's bids for connection. *"When I ask how her day was, I actually listen now,"* Paul shared. *"And when he tells me about something he's excited about, I try to share in that excitement,"* Sarah added.

These small shifts didn't erase their pain overnight, but they laid the groundwork for deeper vulnerability and trust—essential ingredients for rekindling passion.

The Principle of Polarity

While trust and vulnerability are the foundation, passion in a relationship thrives on polarity—the dynamic tension between masculine and feminine energy. Tony Robbins explains that this isn't about gender but about complementary energies that create attraction.

- **Masculine Energy**: Associated with drive, focus, and the desire to lead or protect.
- **Feminine Energy**: Linked to nurturing, creativity, and receptiveness.

In long-term relationships, as partners settle into routines, this polarity often diminishes. Both partners may adopt more neutral roles to manage the demands of daily life, unintentionally dampening the spark that initially drew them together.

Paul and Sarah experienced this firsthand. *"We were stuck in this pattern where everything felt like a negotiation—who's doing the dishes, who's taking the kids to soccer,"* Sarah explained. *"It's like we forgot how to just be with each other."*

To reignite polarity, Robbins suggests intentionally cultivating these energies. For Paul, this meant stepping into a more assertive role, planning date nights and surprising Sarah with thoughtful gestures. For Sarah, it meant leaning into her feminine energy by expressing appreciation for

Paul's efforts and allowing herself to receive his affection without skepticism.

These changes weren't about conforming to stereotypes but about rediscovering the balance that made their connection magnetic.

The Five Love Languages

One of the breakthroughs in Paul and Sarah's journey came when they explored Gary Chapman's concept of the 5 Love Languages. Each person, Chapman explains, has a primary way they express and receive love:

1. **Words of Affirmation**: Expressing love through verbal acknowledgment, compliments, and encouragement.
2. **Quality Time**: Focusing on undivided attention and shared experiences.
3. **Receiving Gifts**: Giving thoughtful tokens that show care and attention.
4. **Acts of Service**: Demonstrating love through helpful actions and support.
5. **Physical Touch**: Communicating affection through physical connection.

When Paul and Sarah identified their love languages, they realized why their previous attempts at connection often fell flat.

"I kept doing things for her—cleaning the house, fixing things—because I thought that's how I showed I cared," Paul admitted. *"But what she really wanted was for me to sit with her and just talk."*

Sarah nodded. *"And I kept giving him compliments, thinking that would make him feel loved. But what he really needed were those acts of service that I sometimes took for granted."*

Understanding their love languages allowed them to speak each other's emotional dialects, creating a sense of connection that had been missing for years.

The Role of Emotional Attunement

At the heart of these tools—vulnerability, polarity, and love languages—is emotional attunement. This is the ability to tune into your partner's feelings, needs, and experiences with empathy and presence.

Research shows that emotionally attuned partners are better equipped to navigate conflicts, address unmet needs, and deepen their bond. Attunement isn't about solving every problem; it's about showing up with compassion and a willingness to understand.

For Paul and Sarah, emotional attunement meant making time to check in with each other regularly. They set aside one evening a week to talk—not about logistics or daily stresses, but about their feelings, dreams, and hopes for the future.

A Path to Reconnection

As Paul and Sarah began practicing these principles, their relationship transformed. The tension and resentment didn't disappear overnight, but their efforts created a new dynamic—one of curiosity, appreciation, and mutual support.

One evening, Sarah shared something that struck Paul deeply. *"I didn't realize how much I missed laughing with you,"* she said. *"It feels good to laugh again."*

Paul smiled. *"Me too,"* he said.

It was a simple exchange, but it captured the essence of their journey. Rebuilding passion isn't about grand gestures or perfect solutions. It's about showing up, day after day, with a commitment to love each other better.

Actionable Steps for Rebuilding Passion

If you're ready to rekindle intimacy and connection in your relationship, here are practical steps to get started:

1. **Respond to Bids for Connection**: Pay attention to the small ways your partner reaches out for attention or support, and respond with engagement.
2. **Rediscover Polarity**: Explore ways to cultivate complementary energies in your relationship. This might

mean planning a surprise for your partner or expressing appreciation for their strengths.

3. **Speak Each Other's Love Language**: Identify your primary love languages and find simple ways to express love in a way your partner understands.
4. **Schedule Time for Emotional Check-Ins**: Set aside regular time to talk about your feelings, dreams, and experiences, free from distractions.

The Gift of Connection

Reigniting passion in a long-term relationship isn't about recapturing what you had in the past—it's about creating something even deeper and more meaningful in the present.

Paul and Sarah's journey reminds us that love isn't static. It's a living, breathing connection that requires care, curiosity, and effort to thrive.

The passion you seek is still there, waiting to be rediscovered. And the path to it begins with a single step—one that you and your partner can take together.

Paul and Sarah's Breakthrough

The room felt lighter, warmer, as Paul and Sarah sat together on the couch. The tension that had once hung heavy between them was gone, replaced by something new—curiosity, perhaps, or maybe a quiet sense of hope.

"It feels different now," Sarah said, her voice softer than I'd ever heard it. *"We're starting to see each other again."*

Paul nodded. *"For the first time in years, I feel like we're really a team."*

Their journey to this moment hadn't been easy, but it had been worth it. And it all began with a simple but transformative realization: they had been speaking different love languages.

Discovering Their Love Languages

When Paul and Sarah first took Gary Chapman's *Love Languages Quiz*, the results surprised them. Sarah's primary love language was *quality time*—uninterrupted moments of connection where she felt truly seen and valued. Paul's, on the other hand, was *words of affirmation*—he felt most loved when Sarah acknowledged and appreciated his efforts.

The problem was clear: they had been expressing love in ways that made sense to them, but not in ways the other could fully receive.

"I thought I was showing her I cared by fixing things around the house, but that's not what she needed," Paul admitted. *"She needed me to just sit with her and be present."*

Sarah smiled. *"And I thought I was showing him love by complimenting him here and there, but he needed more than that. He needed to hear that I appreciated all the things he did for us."*

This understanding was a turning point for both of them. It gave them a framework to express love in ways that felt meaningful and personal, reigniting the emotional connection that had been missing for so long.

Practical Steps Toward Reconnection

Understanding their love languages was only the beginning. Paul and Sarah knew that lasting change required consistent effort, so they committed to a few practical steps to rebuild their relationship.

1. **Dedicated Couple Time**: They agreed to set aside one night a week as *"date night."* No distractions, no talk of work or kids—just time to focus on each other.
2. Their first date night was simple: a walk in the park followed by coffee at a quiet café. *"It wasn't fancy, but it felt special,"* Sarah said. *"It reminded me of when we were first dating."*
3. **Affirming Each Other's Efforts**: Paul made it a point to verbalize his appreciation for Sarah's contributions, whether it was a thoughtful meal or her patience during a stressful day. *"I realized how much it meant to her to hear me say, 'Thank you,'"* he said.
4. Sarah, in turn, started noticing the small ways Paul showed his love—like fixing the leaky faucet or bringing

her a cup of tea without being asked—and made sure to acknowledge them.

5. **Practicing Gratitude**: Each evening, before bed, they shared one thing they were grateful for about each other. *"It felt awkward at first,"* Paul admitted, *"but it helped us focus on the positive instead of dwelling on what wasn't working."*

Rekindling Emotional Intimacy

As they continued these practices, something remarkable began to happen: their emotional bond deepened.

Sarah started looking forward to their weekly date nights, where they would talk about their dreams, their memories, and even their fears. *"It felt like we were peeling back layers,"* she said. *"Like we were getting to know each other all over again."*

Paul noticed a shift in their physical connection, too. *"When we started focusing on each other emotionally, the physical part just... followed,"* he said, a touch of warmth in his voice. *"It wasn't forced. It felt natural again."*

This renewed intimacy wasn't just about the big moments—it was about the small ones, too. A shared laugh over a silly joke. A lingering hug before heading out the door. The simple joy of holding hands during a movie.

The Role of Gratitude

One of the most transformative practices for Paul and Sarah was their nightly gratitude ritual. By ending each day with a moment of appreciation, they shifted their focus from what was lacking to what was abundant in their relationship.

Gratitude, research shows, is a powerful tool for strengthening relationships. It fosters positive emotions, reinforces trust, and creates a sense of connection. For Paul and Sarah, it became a daily reminder of why they chose each other in the first place.

Over time, these small, intentional actions created a ripple effect in Paul and Sarah's relationship. The tension and resentment that once defined their interactions gave way to laughter, tenderness, and a renewed sense of partnership.

"It's not perfect," Paul admitted. *"We still have moments where we slip back into old habits. But now we have tools to get back on track."*

Sarah nodded. *"It's like we've built a new foundation—one that's stronger because we built it together."*

Actionable Tools for Rekindling Passion

If you're looking to strengthen your own relationship, here are a few tools inspired by Paul and Sarah's journey:

1. **Love Languages Quiz**: Take the time to understand your partner's primary love language and find small, daily ways to express love in a way they'll appreciate.
2. **Gratitude Journal Prompts**: Each day, write down one thing you appreciate about your partner. Share these thoughts regularly to build a culture of gratitude.
3. **Dedicated Couple Time**: Set aside regular time for uninterrupted connection, whether it's a weekly date night or a simple evening walk.
4. **Communication Exercises**: Practice active listening and expressing needs constructively. Focus on understanding rather than defending.

The Power of Reconnection

Paul and Sarah's story is a testament to the power of love—not the romanticized version we see in movies, but the real, messy, resilient love that grows stronger through effort and intention.

Reigniting passion isn't about grand gestures or instant fixes. It's about showing up for each other, day after day, with a willingness to listen, to learn, and to love in ways that truly matter.

The spark you're looking for isn't gone—it's still there, waiting to be nurtured. And with every small step you take, you'll find your way back to the connection, intimacy, and joy that brought you together in the first place.

Chapter 6: Financial Freedom: It's Not Too Late to Succeed

Mark's Midlife Money Pivot

Mark sat across from me, his hands clasped tightly together, his shoulders hunched as if he were bracing himself against an invisible weight. His eyes betrayed a mix of emotions: frustration, fear, and a faint glimmer of hope that maybe, just maybe, it wasn't too late to turn things around.

"I don't even know where to begin," he said, shaking his head. *"I've made so many mistakes. It feels like I've dug a hole so deep, I'll never climb out of it."*

Mark was 55 years old, carrying more debt than he cared to admit, and staring down the reality of a retirement account that barely existed. He wasn't living extravagantly. His debt wasn't from luxury vacations or flashy purchases; it was the accumulation of life—medical bills, helping his kids with college, and the occasional unplanned expense that snowballed over time.

The Weight of Feeling *"Behind"*

As Mark shared his story, I could hear the familiar strain of someone who felt trapped by time. *"If I'd started saving earlier, I wouldn't be in this mess,"* he said, his voice tinged with regret. *"I should have known better."*

He paused, his eyes dropping to the floor. *"But I didn't. And now it feels like I've failed—not just myself, but my family."*

Mark's fear wasn't just about numbers in a bank account; it was about what those numbers represented. To him, they symbolized his perceived inadequacy, a lifetime of missed opportunities, and the sinking belief that he was running out of time to make things right.

The Emotional Toll of Financial Stress

Mark's story isn't unique. Financial struggles don't just affect our wallets—they affect our sense of self-worth, our relationships, and even our health. The constant worry about money can lead to sleepless nights, strained communication with loved ones, and a pervasive sense of shame that keeps people stuck in a cycle of avoidance.

For Mark, this shame had become paralyzing. Every time he tried to face his finances, the sheer magnitude of what needed to change overwhelmed him. He would shut down, convincing himself that it was too late to fix anything.

Mark's situation reflects a challenge faced by countless individuals: the feeling of being *"behind"* financially, especially later in life. Whether it's due to unforeseen circumstances, a lack of financial education, or simply the pressures of daily life, many people reach their 50s or 60s and find themselves unprepared for the financial realities ahead.

This feeling of being behind creates a powerful narrative: *I'll never catch up. It's too late to start now. Why even bother?*

But here's the truth: It's never too late. The key isn't trying to undo the past—it's focusing on what you can do today.

Mark's Turning Point

As Mark and I continued talking, I asked him a simple question: *"What would success look like to you?"*

He hesitated, clearly uncomfortable with the idea of imagining success when failure felt so close. But eventually, he said, *"I just want to feel like I have control again. Like I can breathe."*

"That's a great place to start," I told him. *"Because financial freedom isn't about hitting a magic number. It's about creating a plan that gives you confidence and peace of mind."*

Mark nodded, though his skepticism was still visible. *"But how? It feels like there's too much to fix."*

"The good news," I said, *"is that you don't have to fix everything at once. You just need to take the first step."*

The First Step: Facing the Numbers

One of the hardest but most essential steps in Mark's journey was facing his financial reality head-on. Together, we created a clear picture of his income, expenses, debts, and assets. It wasn't easy—there were moments when he winced at the numbers, moments when he wanted to walk away.

But with each piece of data we added, something unexpected happened: the problem started to feel less abstract and more manageable.

"It's not as bad as I thought," he said at one point. *"I mean, it's not great, but at least I know what I'm dealing with."*

This clarity was a turning point for Mark. It shifted his mindset from one of avoidance to one of action.

Breaking the Paralysis

Mark's biggest obstacle wasn't his debt or his savings—it was the paralysis caused by his belief that change was impossible. To combat this, we focused on small, achievable goals:

- **Creating a budget**: Mark learned to track his spending and identify areas where he could cut back without feeling deprived.
- **Building an emergency fund**: He started with a goal of saving $1,000, knowing that even a modest cushion could provide peace of mind.
- **Prioritizing debt repayment**: We created a plan to tackle his smallest debts first, giving him quick wins that built momentum.

Each of these steps gave Mark a sense of control he hadn't felt in years.

The Emotional Shift

As Mark began to see progress, his mindset shifted. The fear and shame that once held him back were replaced by a growing sense of confidence and determination.

"I used to think about money as this thing I could never get right," he said during one of our sessions. *"But now I see it differently. It's not about being perfect—it's about being consistent."*

Mark's progress wasn't just about numbers; it was about reclaiming his sense of agency.

The Gift of Starting Late

One of the most powerful lessons Mark learned was that starting late isn't a failure—it's an opportunity.

"When you start late, you appreciate it more," he said. *"Every step feels like a victory, because you're proving to yourself that it's never too late to change."*

Mark's story reminds us that financial freedom isn't reserved for the young or the wealthy. It's available to anyone who's willing to face their fears, make a plan, and take consistent action.

Mark's journey is proof that financial transformation is possible, no matter your starting point. In the next sections, we'll explore the practical strategies and tools he used to build a brighter financial future—steps that you can take, too.

Because here's the truth: it's not too late. It's never too late to succeed.

Reframing Financial Mindsets

Mark sat in my office, a coffee cup in his hand, staring out the window. His voice carried a mix of hope and disbelief. *"I get it logically—this idea that I can make progress, even now. But I've spent so many years feeling stuck... How do I start seeing things differently?"*

His question cut to the heart of one of the biggest challenges people face when tackling their finances: shifting the mindset that has kept them trapped.

The Scarcity vs. Abundance Mindset

For years, Mark had operated from a place of scarcity. Every decision about money felt like a crisis, a constant calculation of what he couldn't afford and what he was giving up. Scarcity thinking creates a narrative of limitation: *There's never enough. I'll never catch up. It's too late.*

This mindset isn't just about dollars and cents—it's about fear. It keeps us focused on what we lack, paralyzing us with worry and preventing us from seeing opportunities for growth.

To move forward, Mark needed to adopt an abundance mindset, which focuses on possibility and the belief that he could create positive change.

"What would it look like," I asked him, *"if you believed there was enough? Enough time, enough money, enough opportunity to build the life you want?"*

He paused, letting the question sink in. *"I guess... I'd stop feeling so afraid all the time. I'd start looking for ways to make things better instead of just trying to survive."*

That was the shift we needed to make. Abundance isn't about ignoring reality or pretending challenges don't exist—it's about believing you have the power to influence your outcomes.

Compounding Habits: The Power of Small Wins

One of the most liberating concepts I shared with Mark was the idea of compounding habits. This principle, which applies to everything from fitness to finances, is rooted in the idea that small, consistent actions can lead to exponential results over time.

"Think about a snowball rolling down a hill," I told him. *"At first, it's tiny, barely noticeable. But as it rolls, it picks up more snow, growing bigger and faster with each turn. That's how habits work."*

Mark's first step was automating his savings. He set up a direct transfer of $50 from each paycheck into a high-yield savings account. *"It's not much,"* he said, *"but it's a start."*

What he didn't realize was how powerful that small action could become. Over the course of a year, those $50 deposits added up to $1,300—not including interest. More importantly, they built momentum. Seeing his savings grow gave Mark the confidence to take additional steps, like reducing unnecessary expenses and exploring investment opportunities.

Small habits compound not just in their results but in the mindset they create. Each positive action reinforces the belief that progress is possible, creating a virtuous cycle of growth.

Shifting Financial Identity

Mark's progress wasn't just about numbers on a spreadsheet—it was about seeing himself differently. For years, he had carried the identity of someone who was *"bad with money."* This belief shaped his actions, leading to avoidance, guilt, and self-doubt.

To change his financial reality, Mark needed to shift his financial identity. Instead of seeing himself as a passive victim of his circumstances, he began to view himself as a capable steward of money—a person who could make intentional, informed choices.

One of the exercises that helped him was journaling about the kind of financial future he wanted to create. I asked him to write down three statements every day:

1. *I am capable of managing my money wisely.*
2. *I am building a secure and abundant financial future.*
3. *Every small step I take moves me closer to my goals.*

At first, he admitted it felt awkward. *"It's hard to believe those things when I'm still in debt,"* he said.

"But that's the point," I told him. *"You're not just describing your current reality—you're creating a new one."*

Over time, these affirmations helped rewire Mark's self-perception. He began to see himself as someone who could take control of his finances, which motivated him to keep building positive habits.

Financial Leverage: The Bucket System

One of the most practical tools I introduced to Mark was Tony Robbins' *"bucket system"* for managing money. The system divides finances into three main categories:

1. **Savings**: Money set aside for short-term goals, emergencies, and future needs.
2. **Spending**: Funds allocated for daily expenses and discretionary spending.
3. **Investing**: Money dedicated to building long-term wealth and creating financial freedom.

This approach gave Mark clarity and control. By dividing his income into these categories, he could see exactly where his money was going and ensure that every dollar had a purpose.

To start, Mark allocated 10% of his income to savings, 70% to spending, and 20% to investing. These percentages weren't set in stone—they were adjusted as his financial situation improved—but they provided a framework for intentional decision-making.

The Mindset of Progress

As Mark embraced these principles, something remarkable happened: his financial challenges didn't feel as overwhelming anymore.

"It's like I finally have a plan," he said. *"I'm not just reacting to bills or stressing about the future—I'm actually building something."*

This mindset shift was transformative. Instead of seeing his finances as a source of stress, Mark began to see them as an opportunity for growth.

Actionable Steps for Reframing Financial Mindsets

If you're ready to shift your financial mindset, here are some steps to help you get started:

1. **Adopt an Abundance Mindset**: Focus on what's possible, not what's lacking. Reflect on the opportunities and resources available to you right now.
2. **Start Small**: Identify one small, consistent habit you can implement today, like automating savings or tracking expenses.
3. **Affirm Your Financial Identity**: Write down affirmations that reflect the person you want to become, such as, *"I am capable of creating financial freedom."*

4. **Use the Bucket System**: Divide your income into savings, spending, and investing categories. Adjust the percentages based on your goals and current situation.

The Gift of a Renewed Mindset

Mark's story is a testament to the power of reframing how we think about money. It's not about perfection—it's about progress.

When you shift your mindset from scarcity to abundance, from fear to possibility, you unlock the ability to take control of your financial future. And no matter where you're starting from, that future is within reach.

Mark's Financial Turnaround

Mark's journey toward financial freedom began on a quiet Sunday afternoon. With a cup of coffee in hand and a notebook open on the kitchen table, he faced the reality he had avoided for years. His financial documents were spread out before him—bills, credit card statements, and a blank spreadsheet ready to capture the numbers that had weighed on him for so long.

"I was scared," he admitted later. *"But I knew that if I didn't take control now, I never would."*

Taking Stock of Fixed Expenses

The first step was identifying his fixed expenses. Mark wrote down every recurring cost—from the obvious, like rent and utilities, to the less noticeable subscriptions that had quietly drained his account over the years.

"I couldn't believe how much I was spending on things I didn't even use," he said. *"Streaming services, old gym memberships, even that magazine subscription I forgot to cancel."*

By trimming unnecessary expenses, Mark freed up an additional $200 per month. It wasn't a fortune, but it was a start.

Negotiating Debt Repayment Plans

Next, Mark tackled his debts. Instead of letting the overwhelming totals paralyze him, he reached out to his creditors to negotiate repayment plans. It wasn't an easy conversation, but the results were worth it.

"I was honest with them," he explained. *"I told them I wanted to pay what I owed but needed terms I could actually manage. Most of them were surprisingly willing to work with me."*

Mark created a simple *"Debt Snowball Worksheet"* to prioritize his repayments. He focused on paying off his smallest debts first, gaining momentum and confidence with each success.

"Knocking out that first credit card felt amazing," he said. *"It gave me the motivation to keep going."*

Creating a Budget Aligned with Priorities

Mark's budget wasn't about deprivation—it was about alignment. He wanted his spending to reflect his values and goals, not just his obligations.

Together, we created a budget that balanced his needs and priorities. He allocated a percentage of his income to essentials like housing and food, a portion to debt repayment, and a smaller amount to savings and investments.

"This was the first time in my life I felt like I was in control of my money, instead of the other way around," he said.

Building a Financial Foundation

With his budget in place, Mark began exploring tools and strategies to rebuild his financial foundation.

1. **Automatic Savings Plans**: Mark set up a direct deposit to transfer a small amount of his paycheck into a high-yield savings account. *"It was only $50 at first,"* he said, *"but seeing that account grow each month gave me so much hope."*
2. **Micro-Investments**: Using beginner-friendly investing apps, Mark started investing spare change from everyday purchases. *"It wasn't much, but it was a step toward building wealth instead of just getting by,"* he explained.

3. **A Part-Time Side Hustle**: Mark leveraged his skills to take on freelance writing projects in his spare time. The extra income allowed him to accelerate his debt repayment and contribute more to his savings.

The Emotional Transformation

As Mark's financial situation improved, so did his emotional well-being.

"I can't even describe the relief I felt when I paid off my first big loan," he said. *"It was like this weight I'd been carrying for years just disappeared."*

Mark's newfound confidence extended beyond his finances. He began setting long-term goals, like saving for a trip with his family and eventually purchasing a small home.

"Money used to feel like this impossible mountain to climb," he reflected. *"Now, it feels like a tool—a way to build the life I want, not something holding me back."*

The reduced stress also strengthened Mark's relationships. *"I used to snap at my wife whenever we talked about money,"* he admitted. *"Now, those conversations feel more like teamwork. We're on the same page, working toward the same goals."*

Practical Tools for Your Financial Turnaround

If you're ready to take control of your finances, here are some tools to help you get started:

1. **Debt Snowball Worksheet**: List your debts from smallest to largest. Focus on paying off the smallest debt first while making minimum payments on the others. Use each success as motivation to tackle the next.
2. **Savings Tracker**: Create a visual tracker to monitor your progress. Whether it's a bar graph or a jar you fill with tokens, seeing your savings grow can be incredibly motivating.
3. **Beginner-Friendly Investing Apps**: Apps like Acorns or Robinhood make it easy to start investing, even with small amounts. These tools help demystify investing and make it accessible to anyone.

A New Chapter

Mark's financial turnaround wasn't about winning the lottery or discovering a secret formula. It was about taking small, intentional steps every day.

"Looking back, I wish I'd started sooner," he said. *"But I'm proud of what I've accomplished. And I know that no matter what happens, I have the tools and mindset to keep moving forward."*

Mark's story is a powerful reminder that financial freedom isn't just about dollars and cents—it's about reclaiming your sense of control, confidence, and possibility.

No matter where you're starting from, your financial future is still yours to create. And the best time to start? It's today.

Bonus Chapter: A Personal Gift—Simple Strategies for Building Financial Confidence

Claim Your Free Audiobook Bonus

To gain access to the audiobook version follow this link:

https://tinyurl.com/more-fuel

A Balanced, Long-Term Approach

The idea for this chapter came to me on an evening walk, the kind where your mind drifts freely between the weight of the day and the clarity of new ideas. As I passed a park bathed in the golden light of dusk, I thought about how seasons change—not just in nature, but in life and, yes, in the markets.

Investing has often been portrayed as an intimidating world, one where only experts thrive. But over the years, I've learned that some of the most effective strategies are also the simplest. And what I'm about to share isn't financial advice—it's a personal gift, a collection of principles that have guided me toward financial confidence and a sense of control over my future.

Understanding Seasonal Investments

One of the most intriguing concepts I've come across in my investing journey is the idea of seasonal trends. Just as certain times of the year bring predictable weather patterns, the stock market also moves in cycles influenced by historical trends and economic rhythms.

For example, the retail sector often sees a boost in late fall and early winter, thanks to holiday shopping. Similarly, energy stocks may perform better during the colder months when heating demand rises. The *Stock Trader's Almanac*, a resource I've come to rely on, highlights these patterns and offers a roadmap for understanding market seasonality.

The beauty of seasonal investments is that they allow you to make informed decisions based on historical data, reducing the guesswork and emotional volatility that often come with investing.

One year, I decided to test this principle by focusing on consumer discretionary stocks during the holiday season. Guided by research, I identified companies likely to benefit from increased holiday spending. By the end of the season, I had not only grown my portfolio but also gained confidence in my ability to anticipate market movements.

Seasonal investing isn't about trying to time the market—it's about understanding its natural ebb and flow and positioning yourself to benefit from it.

Balancing Growth with Stability

While seasonal investments can offer exciting opportunities, they're just one piece of the puzzle. True financial confidence comes from balancing growth-oriented strategies with a foundation of stability.

For me, that foundation includes dividend stocks and index funds—two straightforward, low-risk investment vehicles that provide consistent returns over time.

1. **Dividend Stocks**: These are shares of companies that regularly distribute a portion of their profits to shareholders. Think of them as the steady heartbeat of your portfolio, providing income even when markets are unpredictable.
2. I remember the first time I received a dividend payment. It wasn't a large amount, but it felt like a win—a tangible reward for taking that step toward investing. Over time, as I reinvested those dividends, they grew, creating a compounding effect that added significant value to my portfolio.
3. **Index Funds**: These funds track the performance of a market index, such as the S&P 500, offering diversification and reducing the risks associated with picking individual stocks.

When I first started investing, I didn't have the time or expertise to analyze dozens of companies. Index funds became my go-to choice for long-term growth, allowing me to benefit from the overall performance of the market without the stress of active trading.

Balancing these two strategies—dividends for stability and index funds for growth—has provided me with a sense of financial security, even during volatile market conditions.

Tools and Resources for Research

Building confidence in investing starts with equipping yourself with the right tools. Here are a few that have been invaluable in my journey:

1. **The *Stock Trader's Almanac***: A treasure trove of historical data and seasonal trends, this book has helped me identify patterns and plan my investments with greater precision.
2. **Online Seasonal Analysis Tools**: Websites like Equity Clock and StockCharts provide free resources for analyzing seasonal trends in specific sectors and indices.
3. **Financial Newsletters and Forums**: Subscribing to reputable newsletters or joining investing forums can provide insights from seasoned investors, helping you make informed decisions.

These tools aren't about guaranteeing success—they're about empowering you to take control of your financial journey.

The Power of Long-Term Thinking

One of the greatest lessons I've learned about investing is the importance of patience. Markets will rise and fall, often unpredictably. But over time, consistent, well-informed decisions yield rewards far greater than short-term speculation.

When I look back on my investing journey, the moments that stand out aren't the times I made quick gains—they're the times I stayed the course, trusting in the principles I'd built my strategy on.

I think about the year I committed to reinvesting all my dividends, even when I was tempted to withdraw them for immediate needs. That decision, small as it seemed at the time, led to exponential growth that continues to benefit me today.

A Personal Invitation

This chapter isn't just about strategies—it's about a mindset. It's about seeing investing not as a gamble, but as a way to participate in the growth of the world around you. It's about trusting that small, consistent actions can lead to transformative results.

So as you consider your own financial journey, I invite you to embrace these principles. Start with one step—a seasonal investment, a dividend stock, or a commitment to learning more about the markets.

Because no matter where you're starting from, the path to financial confidence is within reach. And every step you take brings you closer to the life you've always wanted.

Three Simple Strategies to Get Started

It was a crisp November evening when I first discovered the power of keeping investment strategies simple. I had spent hours reading articles and analyzing trends, my mind spinning with the sheer complexity of options. Overwhelmed, I stepped outside for a moment of clarity. As the cool air filled my lungs, I remembered something a mentor once told me: *"The simplest plans are often the most effective."*

That evening, I decided to refine my approach to investing—not by trying to master every intricate strategy but by focusing on a few core principles. Today, I want to share three simple strategies that helped me build confidence and stability in my financial journey.

1. Seasonal Investments: Harnessing Market Cycles

Every industry has its rhythms, much like the changing of the seasons. Recognizing these patterns can give you an edge, especially when you're just starting. One of the most reliable examples is the tendency for consumer discretionary and tech stocks to perform well in the fourth quarter, driven by holiday spending and end-of-year business investments.

Take a moment to imagine the bustling energy of the holiday season. Stores are crowded, online shopping carts are overflowing, and companies like Amazon, Apple, and Target are seeing their busiest months. Historically, this translates into strong performance for stocks in these sectors during Q4.

Actionable Plan:

- **Research Seasonal Patterns**: Use tools like the *Stock Trader's Almanac* or online resources to identify historical trends for specific sectors.
- **Start Small with ETFs or Mutual Funds**: Instead of picking individual stocks, consider exchange-traded funds (ETFs) that focus on consumer discretionary or tech sectors. For example, an ETF like the Consumer Discretionary Select Sector SPDR Fund (XLY) provides exposure to multiple companies in the sector, reducing risk.
- **Time Your Investments**: If you're planning to invest during a high-performing season, consider dollar-cost averaging—investing a fixed amount at regular intervals to smooth out market fluctuations.

By aligning your investments with seasonal trends, you can take advantage of predictable market cycles without overcomplicating your strategy.

2. Dividend Investing: Building Passive Income

When I received my first dividend payment, it wasn't much—just a few dollars. But the feeling was unforgettable. For the first time, I realized that my money could work for me, generating income without requiring constant effort.

That small payment was a spark, igniting a deeper interest in dividend investing.

Dividend-paying stocks are like reliable friends: steady, dependable, and rewarding over time. Companies like Procter & Gamble and Coca-Cola have a long history of paying consistent dividends, making them excellent choices for investors seeking stability and cash flow.

The beauty of dividend investing lies in its compounding effect. By reinvesting your dividends, you allow your earnings to generate even more income, creating a snowball effect that grows larger with each passing year.

Actionable Plan:

- **Research Strong Dividend Companies**: Look for companies with a track record of consistent dividend payments. Websites like Dividend.com or tools within brokerage platforms can help identify reliable options.
- **Focus on Dividend Growth**: Prioritize companies that not only pay dividends but also have a history of increasing their payouts over time.
- **Reinvest Your Dividends**: Many brokerage accounts offer an automatic dividend reinvestment plan (DRIP), allowing your earnings to be reinvested without additional effort.

Over time, even modest investments in dividend-paying stocks can become a reliable source of passive income, providing financial stability and freedom.

3. The Rule of Cash Reserves: Flexibility and Stability

One of the most valuable lessons I've learned about investing is the importance of keeping a portion of your portfolio in cash or cash-equivalent reserves. While it might be tempting to go *"all in"* on higher-yield investments, having cash on hand provides flexibility to seize opportunities and weather unexpected downturns.

During the early months of the pandemic, I saw firsthand the value of this approach. Markets were in freefall, and many investors were forced to sell at a loss to cover short-term needs. Because I had cash reserves, I was able to stay calm, avoid panic selling, and even take advantage of discounted stocks during the recovery.

Actionable Plan:

- **Set Aside 10–20% in Cash Equivalents**: Keep a portion of your investment funds in stable, liquid assets like short-term treasury ETFs, money market funds, or high-yield savings accounts.
- **Use Cash for Opportunities**: When markets dip or an attractive investment opportunity arises, your cash reserves give you the ability to act quickly.

- **Maintain Stability**: Knowing you have a financial safety net reduces stress and allows you to stick to your long-term investment plan without being derailed by market volatility.

This strategy isn't about timing the market—it's about being prepared, confident, and adaptable no matter what comes your way.

A Path Toward Confidence

These three strategies—seasonal investments, dividend investing, and maintaining cash reserves—aren't about achieving overnight wealth. They're about building a foundation of confidence and stability that allows you to grow steadily over time.

As you begin implementing these ideas, remember that progress is more important than perfection. Each small step you take is a step toward greater financial empowerment.

Whether it's researching seasonal trends, buying your first dividend stock, or setting aside a portion of your income in cash reserves, every action brings you closer to a future where your money works for you—not the other way around.

Because financial confidence isn't just about numbers—it's about the peace of mind that comes from knowing you're building something meaningful, one step at a time.

The Importance of Consistency

It was a late afternoon in spring when I had a conversation with an old friend that shifted my perspective on financial growth. We were sitting on his porch, watching the sun dip below the horizon, when he said something that stuck with me: *"The best investment isn't always the smartest or the most profitable—it's the one you stick with."*

Those words carried a truth that resonates deeply in the world of personal finance: consistency is king. No matter how much you start with or how little you think you know, committing to steady, regular contributions can create remarkable results over time.

The Power of Regular Contributions

When I first started investing, I was intimidated by the idea of needing large sums of money to make any real progress. But I quickly realized that small, consistent actions often yield the greatest rewards.

One of the simplest yet most powerful tools in my financial arsenal has been automation. By setting up automated transfers into my savings and investment accounts, I removed the temptation to skip a contribution or *"wait until next month."*

Every paycheck, a portion of my income goes directly into my financial goals. Some months it's a larger amount, some months it's smaller, but it always happens. Over time, those small, steady contributions add up to something significant.

Consider this: if you invest just $100 a month into an index fund with an average annual return of 7%, you'll have over $24,000 after 10 years. Increase that amount to $200 a month, and you're looking at nearly $50,000. The key isn't the amount—it's the consistency.

A Simple Allocation Framework

To keep things manageable and aligned with my financial goals, I developed a straightforward allocation framework. Think of it as a roadmap for how to divide your investments based on your priorities and risk tolerance.

1. **50% to Stable, Dividend-Paying Stocks or ETFs**: These investments act as the foundation of your portfolio, providing steady income and stability over time. Dividend-paying stocks like Johnson & Johnson or ETFs like the Vanguard Dividend Appreciation ETF (VIG) are great options for this category. Reinvesting the dividends from these investments creates a powerful compounding effect, growing your wealth even faster.
2. **30% to Growth Opportunities**: This portion is dedicated to investments with higher growth potential, such as seasonal patterns or specific sectors like technology or clean energy.

For example, during Q4, I often allocate part of this category to consumer discretionary ETFs, taking advantage of increased holiday spending. The goal here isn't to chase trends but to thoughtfully explore opportunities for growth.

3. **20% to Cash Reserves or Short-Term Investments**: This allocation provides flexibility and stability, ensuring you're prepared for emergencies or able to seize new opportunities. Short-term treasury ETFs or high-yield savings accounts are excellent options for this category.

Having cash reserves isn't just practical—it's empowering. It gives you the confidence to navigate market fluctuations without fear.

Staying Consistent with Tools and Resources

Consistency is easier when you have the right tools to support your efforts. Here are a few that have made a difference in my financial journey:

1. **Free Brokerage Platforms**: Companies like Fidelity, Vanguard, and Robinhood offer user-friendly platforms with low or no fees, making it easy to manage your investments.
2. **Robo-Advisors**: For those who prefer a hands-off approach, robo-advisors like Betterment or Wealthfront provide automated investment management based on your goals and risk tolerance.

3. **Investment Apps**: Apps like Acorns or Stash round up your everyday purchases and invest the spare change, making it effortless to build your portfolio over time.

These tools remove barriers and simplify the process, allowing you to focus on consistency rather than complexity.

The Emotional Rewards of Consistency

As I've watched my portfolio grow over the years, I've realized that the greatest reward isn't just the financial progress—it's the sense of control and confidence that comes with knowing I'm building something meaningful.

Consistency also changes your mindset. Instead of feeling overwhelmed by the enormity of financial goals, you start to see them as achievable, one step at a time. Each contribution, no matter how small, becomes a victory—a tangible reminder that you're moving forward.

A Journey Built on Steady Steps

One of my favorite metaphors for consistency comes from hiking. Imagine standing at the base of a mountain, looking up at the summit. It's easy to feel intimidated by how far you have to go. But when you focus on putting one foot in front of the other, step by step, you eventually find yourself at the top.

The same is true for building financial confidence. It's not about making huge leaps or finding the perfect strategy—it's about committing to steady, intentional actions that move you closer to your goals.

Practical Steps for Consistency

If you're ready to make consistency the cornerstone of your financial journey, here are some steps to get started:

1. **Automate Your Contributions**: Set up automatic transfers to your savings or investment accounts. Start with an amount you're comfortable with and increase it as your financial situation improves.
2. **Follow a Simple Allocation Framework**: Use the 50/30/20 rule to guide your investments, adjusting the percentages as needed based on your goals.
3. **Track Your Progress**: Use a spreadsheet, app, or visual tracker to monitor your growth. Seeing the results of your consistency reinforces your commitment.
4. **Celebrate Small Wins**: Every milestone—whether it's paying off a debt, hitting a savings goal, or making your first investment—is worth celebrating.

A Legacy of Growth

As I reflect on my financial journey, I'm reminded of the ripple effect consistency creates. It doesn't just impact your finances—it transforms your mindset, builds your confidence, and inspires those around you.

When you commit to regular, intentional actions, you're not just building a portfolio—you're building a legacy. And that legacy starts with a single step, repeated again and again, until it becomes the foundation of a life you've always wanted.

Part 3:
Leave Your Mark and Live Fully

CHAPTER 7:

LIVING WITH PURPOSE, NOT REGRET

David's Turning Point

David sat across from me, his hands clasped tightly as if trying to hold himself together. At 60 years old, he looked like a man who had carried too much for too long. His shoulders slumped under the weight of his regrets, and his eyes held the dull ache of someone replaying the same *"what ifs"* over and over again.

"I don't know where to start," he said finally, his voice heavy with exhaustion. *"I look back, and all I can see are the mistakes I made. The chances I didn't take. It feels like it's too late to do anything that really matters now."*

David's story is one I've heard countless times. It's the story of someone who has spent decades building a life only to look up one day and wonder if they built the right one. His regrets weren't just about missed opportunities—they were about the meaning he feared he'd never find.

Consumed by Regret

David's regrets fell into two main categories: his career and his relationships.

In his career, he'd played it safe, sticking with a job that paid the bills but never inspired him. *"I had dreams,"* he said quietly, almost as if confessing a secret. *"I wanted to start my own business, something creative, something I could pour my heart into. But I was too afraid to take the risk. Now, I look back, and I wonder what could have been."*

In his relationships, he carried the guilt of time not spent. *"I was so focused on providing for my family that I missed so much,"* he admitted, his voice cracking. *"I missed birthdays, school plays, the little moments that really matter. And now that my kids are grown, I can't get that time back."*

Regret is a heavy burden because it feels irreversible. For David, it wasn't just about the past—it was about the story he told himself about what those missed opportunities meant. To him, they meant failure.

The Emotional Weight of Regret

The weight of regret doesn't just live in the mind—it seeps into every part of life. For David, it showed up in his relationships with his family, his work, and even his health. He often felt paralyzed, unable to move forward because he was so consumed by what he had left behind.

"I wake up in the middle of the night," he told me, *"thinking about all the things I should have done differently. I can't stop blaming myself."*

This cycle of guilt and self-blame is a common trap. Regret convinces us that we're defined by our past mistakes, that we've missed our chance to make a difference. But the truth is, as long as we're still here, it's never too late to start living with purpose.

David's story resonates because it touches on a universal struggle: the tension between the life we've lived and the life we still have time to create. Regret is a natural part of being human. It's impossible to go through life without making choices we later question or missing opportunities we later wish we'd taken.

But while regret can feel like a prison, it doesn't have to define us. Viktor Frankl, in his seminal work *Man's Search for Meaning,* wrote that life is never made unbearable by circumstances alone but by the lack of meaning and purpose.

For David—and for anyone consumed by regret—the key wasn't erasing the past. It was learning to pivot from the past to an intentional present.

The first step in David's journey was acknowledging the emotions he'd been burying for years. *"You don't have to ignore your regrets,"* I told him. *"But you don't have to carry them like a backpack full of stones, either. What if, instead of seeing them as failures, you saw them as lessons?"*

At first, he resisted. *"How can you find a lesson in wasting your life?"* he asked bitterly.

I let the question hang in the air for a moment before replying. *"Because your regrets show you what matters to you. The fact that you regret not spending more time with your kids means you value connection. The fact that you regret not pursuing your dreams means you still have dreams worth chasing."*

That idea—that regret could be a teacher instead of a tormentor—sparked something in David. He didn't let go of his guilt overnight, but he began to see it differently.

The Challenge of Moving Forward

For David, the biggest challenge was shifting his focus from *"what was"* to *"what could be."* Regret keeps us anchored in the past, but purpose is rooted in the present. It's about asking not, *What did I miss?* but *What can I do now?*

One of the exercises that helped David was writing a letter to his younger self. In it, he acknowledged the mistakes he'd made but also offered himself forgiveness. *"I wrote that I did the best I could with what I knew at the time,"* he said. *"And for the first time, I started to believe it."*

The next step was envisioning the life he wanted to create moving forward. He started small, setting goals that aligned with his values. He reached out to his kids for more frequent phone calls and visits. He began exploring creative hobbies, dabbling in photography—a passion he'd left behind years ago.

A Glimpse of Redemption

One day, David shared a story that brought a smile to his face. *"I was out taking photos at a park, just playing around with my camera,"* he said. *"And this little girl came up to me and asked if I'd take a picture of her and her dog. She was so excited when I showed her the photo, and she said, 'You're really good at this!'"*

He paused, his expression softening. *"It made me realize... maybe it's not too late to do something that matters. Maybe I can still make an impact."*

That moment didn't erase David's regrets, but it reminded him that purpose isn't about perfection. It's about presence.

David's story is a reminder that our past doesn't have to dictate our future. Regret may whisper that you've missed your chance, but purpose shouts that your best days are still ahead.

If you've ever felt consumed by what you didn't do, take heart. Living with purpose isn't about rewriting your history—it's about reclaiming your now. And as long as you're here, there's time to make an impact.

Because the life you've lived isn't the final draft. It's just the opening chapter of the story you're still writing.

Turning Regret into Purpose

David's story didn't end with his regrets—it was just the beginning. As he sat in my office, wrestling with the weight of his past, I could see a spark of something else: a quiet determination.

"I don't want to spend the rest of my life feeling this way," he said finally. *"But I don't know where to start."*

"You've already started," I told him. *"Admitting that you want change is the first step. Now, it's about deciding what comes next."*

Shifting Focus: Future-Oriented Thinking

One of the most powerful ways to move past regret is by shifting your focus from the past to the future. Regret keeps us anchored in what we can't change, but purpose propels us toward what we can create.

I asked David to picture himself five years from now. *"What do you want your life to look like?"* I asked. *"What kind of relationships, experiences, and impact do you want to have?"*

At first, he hesitated. *"I've spent so much time thinking about what I've lost,"* he said, *"I don't even know how to imagine what's possible."*

"That's okay," I assured him. *"Start small. What's one thing you'd love to do that would make you feel proud?"*

After a moment, he said, *"I'd like to rebuild my relationship with my kids. I want them to see me as someone who shows up for them, not just someone who's sorry for the past."*

That simple goal became David's first step toward future-oriented thinking. Instead of dwelling on what he'd missed, he began focusing on what he could do today to create the future he wanted.

Leverage: The Pain of Inaction, the Pleasure of Action

To sustain meaningful change, it's essential to find leverage—a principle Tony Robbins describes as associating pain with inaction and pleasure with purposeful action.

For David, the pain of staying stuck in regret was already clear. *"I don't want to wake up in ten years and realize I wasted even more time,"* he said.

I asked him to dig deeper. *"What's at stake if you don't make a change?"*

He looked down, his voice barely above a whisper. *"My relationships. My self-respect. My chance to leave something meaningful behind."*

Then, I encouraged him to imagine the flip side: the pleasure of purposeful action. *"What would it feel like to take steps toward the life you want?"*

A small smile crept onto his face. *"It would feel... freeing. Like I'm finally doing something that matters."*

This exercise helped David find his motivation—not just to move away from pain but to move toward purpose.

The Power of a North Star Goal

Purpose is most powerful when it's tied to a *"north star"* goal—an overarching vision that provides clarity and direction. For David, that goal became clear as we continued our conversation.

"I want to be the kind of person my kids are proud of," he said. *"Someone who makes a difference, even in small ways."*

With that goal in mind, we broke it down into actionable steps:

1. **Rebuilding Relationships**: David committed to reaching out to his kids regularly—not with apologies for the past, but with genuine interest in their lives today.
2. **Making an Impact**: He began volunteering at a local community center, mentoring young people who were navigating challenges similar to those he'd faced.

3. **Pursuing Passion Projects**: David rediscovered his love for woodworking, creating small gifts for his family and friends—a tangible expression of his commitment to connection.

This north star goal didn't erase David's regrets, but it gave him a way to channel them into something meaningful.

Lessons from Viktor Frankl

David's journey echoes the teachings of Viktor Frankl, who wrote that meaning is found not in what happens to us but in how we respond. In *Man's Search for Meaning,* Frankl emphasizes the importance of intentional action and service to others as pathways to purpose.

For David, these principles became a guiding light. By focusing on what he could give—to his family, his community, and himself—he began to feel a sense of fulfillment he hadn't experienced in years.

Transforming Regret into Fuel

As David leaned into his purpose, he noticed an unexpected shift. *"I used to think about my regrets as this heavy weight I had to carry,"* he said. *"But now, they feel more like fuel—like reminders of why it's so important to keep moving forward."*

This transformation didn't happen overnight. There were moments when old feelings of guilt crept back in, when he questioned whether he was doing enough. But each time, he returned to his north star goal, using it as a compass to guide his actions.

"I can't change what happened," he said one day, *"but I can decide what happens next. And that's enough."*

Practical Tools for Turning Regret into Purpose

If you're ready to transform your regrets into a source of purpose, here are some steps to help you get started:

1. **Identify a North Star Goal**: Think about what matters most to you. What legacy do you want to leave? Let this goal serve as your guiding vision.
2. **Leverage Pain and Pleasure**: Reflect on the consequences of staying stuck in regret and the rewards of taking purposeful action. Use this contrast to fuel your motivation.
3. **Break It Down**: Turn your north star goal into actionable steps. Start small, focusing on one thing you can do today to move closer to your vision.
4. **Focus on Service**: Look for ways to contribute to others, whether through volunteering, mentoring, or acts of kindness. Purpose often grows through connection.

The Path Ahead

David's story is a testament to the power of choosing purpose over regret. It's not about erasing the past—it's about using it to inform a future that's meaningful and fulfilling.

As he continued his journey, David found that his regrets didn't disappear—they transformed. They became reminders of what he valued, motivating him to live with greater intention and heart.

Your regrets don't have to define you. They can become the foundation for something beautiful—a life built not on *"what was"* but on *"what can be."* And with every step you take toward that life, you'll discover that purpose isn't a destination. It's a way of being.

David's Journey to Legacy

It was a crisp autumn morning when David walked into my office with a different energy. His posture was taller, his eyes clearer. Something had shifted. *"I've been thinking,"* he said, sitting down with a thoughtful expression. *"Maybe my life isn't about making up for the past. Maybe it's about creating something meaningful moving forward."*

This was the turning point we'd been working toward—a moment when David began to see his regrets not as chains, but as stepping stones.

Transforming Perspective: Identifying Core Values

The first step in David's transformation was uncovering his core values—the principles that mattered most to him and had been quietly shaping his sense of purpose all along.

During one session, I asked him to list what he valued most. At first, his answers were surface-level: financial security, stability, success. But as we dug deeper, a clearer picture began to emerge.

"Family," he said, his voice softening. *"I've always cared about my family, even when I didn't show it the way I should have."*

He added mentorship to the list, explaining how much he had enjoyed coaching younger colleagues in his career. Finally, he named creativity—a passion he'd all but forgotten but had recently rediscovered through his photography and woodworking projects.

These values became the foundation for the next chapter of David's life. Instead of dwelling on what he hadn't done, he began focusing on how he could live these values moving forward.

"I can't change the time I missed with my kids," he said, *"but I can show up for them now. I can show them what matters to me."*

Practical Steps Toward Purpose

With his core values in mind, David crafted a vision for his next decade—one rooted in connection, contribution, and creativity. Together, we broke that vision into actionable steps, creating a roadmap that felt both inspiring and achievable.

1. Volunteering in a Mentorship Program

David's love for mentorship led him to volunteer at a local organization that paired experienced professionals with young adults navigating their careers.

"It feels good to give back," he said after his first session. *"These kids remind me of myself at that age—so eager to learn, but unsure of where to start. Helping them find their way makes me feel like all my own struggles had a purpose."*

2. Reconnecting with Family

One of David's most significant steps was reaching out to his estranged brother, whom he hadn't spoken to in nearly a decade. *"We had a falling out years ago,"* he explained, *"and I always told myself I'd fix it someday. But someday never came."*

With a mix of nerves and determination, David picked up the phone and made the call. The conversation wasn't perfect—it was awkward and emotional—but it was a start. Over time, they began rebuilding their relationship, finding common ground in shared memories and a mutual desire to move forward.

3. Pursuing a Lifelong Passion for Art

Creativity had always been a part of David's life, but it had taken a back seat to work and responsibilities. Now, he made it a priority.

He enrolled in a community art class, picking up a paintbrush for the first time in decades. *"I was nervous at first,"* he admitted, *"but once I started, it was like a part of me woke up. I'd forgotten how much I love creating."*

His art became more than a hobby—it became a way to connect with others. He gifted his paintings to family members, joined local art shows, and even started teaching a beginner class at the community center.

Renewed Vitality and Purpose

As David leaned into these actions, something remarkable happened: his regrets began to fade. They didn't disappear entirely, but they no longer held the same power over him.

"I feel alive again," he said during one of our later sessions. *"It's not that I've forgotten my mistakes—it's that I've finally found a way to move beyond them."*

David's renewed sense of purpose also had a ripple effect on his relationships. His kids noticed the change in him, describing him as more present and engaged than ever before. His brother, once distant, became a regular part of his life. And through his mentorship and art, David found a sense of connection to his community that he'd never experienced before.

Practical Tools: From Values to Actions

David's journey was guided by a simple but powerful exercise we called the *"Values to Actions"* worksheet. This tool helped him align his daily activities with his long-term goals, ensuring that his actions reflected his priorities.

Here's how you can use it:

1. **Identify Your Core Values**: List the principles that matter most to you. Think about what brings you joy, fulfillment, and a sense of meaning.
2. **Set a North Star Goal**: Based on your values, define a long-term vision for your life. What impact do you want to make?
3. **Break It Down**: Create actionable steps that align with your values and goal. Start small—one phone call, one class, one act of kindness.
4. **Reflect and Adjust**: Regularly revisit your actions to ensure they align with your values. Adjust as needed to stay on course.

Legacy in Action

David's story is a testament to the transformative power of living with purpose. By identifying his values, setting a vision, and taking consistent action, he not only alleviated his regrets but also created a legacy that reflected his best self.

"I used to think legacy was about what you leave behind," he said. *"But now I realize it's about how you live every day. It's about the love you give, the connections you build, and the passion you share with the world."*

David's journey reminds us that it's never too late to rewrite our story. No matter where you're starting from, you have the power to create a life of meaning and fulfillment.

Your legacy isn't written in the past—it's created in the present, one purposeful action at a time.

CHAPTER 8:
CONNECTING DEEPER WITH FAMILY AND FRIENDS

Tom's Journey to Rebuilding Family Ties

Tom sat in his favorite armchair, staring at a photo of his family from years ago. The frame was dusted with age, much like the memories it held. In the photo, his two kids were young, their laughter frozen in time, and his wife stood beside him, radiant and full of life. But as he looked at the smiling faces, a wave of sadness washed over him.

At 62, Tom felt more alone than he ever had. His children were adults now, busy with their own lives, and his wife had passed away five years earlier. His days felt long and empty, filled with reminders of what once was and regrets about what he'd let slip away.

"I don't even know where to start," he admitted during our first conversation. *"I've drifted so far from my kids, and my*

old friends... well, they've moved on. It feels like the bridges I need to cross have burned down."

Tom's story isn't uncommon. Many people find themselves realizing, often too late, that life's busyness has quietly built walls between them and the people they care about most.

Drifting Apart

Tom spoke about his children with a mix of pride and longing. His son, Eric, was a software engineer in Seattle, and his daughter, Claire, had recently opened her own bakery in New York. *"They're doing so well,"* he said, *"but I barely know what's going on in their lives. We talk on holidays, and even then, it feels... strained."*

As he shared more, it became clear that Tom's distance from his kids wasn't just physical—it was emotional. Over the years, he had thrown himself into work, convincing himself that providing for his family was enough. *"I thought I was doing the right thing,"* he said, shaking his head. *"But now I see that I missed so much. And I don't know if they'd even want me in their lives again."*

Tom's struggles extended to his friendships as well. He'd lost touch with close friends, too busy with work and family obligations to nurture those connections. *"It feels like I blinked, and they were gone,"* he said. *"I don't even know how to reach out without it feeling awkward."*

Tom's experience highlights a universal challenge: maintaining relationships amidst the busyness and emotional distance of adult life. It's easy to let weeks turn into months and months into years, assuming there will always be time to reconnect. But when the silence grows too loud, it can feel impossible to bridge the gap.

Feelings of guilt, fear, and uncertainty often hold people back. Tom worried that his kids resented him for not being more present when they were younger. He feared rejection if he reached out to old friends, imagining awkward conversations or, worse, no response at all.

But what Tom didn't realize—what so many people don't—is that most relationships can be rebuilt with intention and effort.

Finding the Courage to Start

"I don't think it's too late," I told Tom during our session. *"But it's going to take courage. Rebuilding relationships means showing up, even when it feels uncomfortable. Are you willing to try?"*

He nodded hesitantly. *"I want to,"* he said. *"But I don't know where to begin."*

We started small. I asked him to write letters to his children—not to send, but to help him process his emotions and clarify what he wanted to say. In those letters, he apologized for the times he'd been absent, expressed his pride in who they'd become, and shared his desire to reconnect.

"It was hard," he admitted later. *"But it also felt good to finally put it into words."*

The next step was reaching out. Tom decided to start with a simple text to each of his kids, letting them know he was thinking of them and asking about their lives. *"It felt awkward,"* he said, *"but they both replied. And that gave me the courage to keep going."*

Rebuilding Bridges

Tom began calling his children more often, learning to ask open-ended questions instead of offering unsolicited advice. He listened without judgment as they shared their challenges and triumphs.

With Eric, he found common ground in their love of technology, even asking for advice on setting up a smart home system. With Claire, he discovered a shared interest in cooking, trading recipes and tips for her bakery.

"I feel like I'm getting to know them all over again," he said, his voice filled with gratitude. *"And the best part is, they seem to want that too."*

Tom also reached out to an old friend, Peter, who he hadn't spoken to in over a decade. *"I thought he'd brush me off,"*

Tom confessed. *"But he was thrilled to hear from me. We ended up talking for hours, and now we're planning to meet for coffee next week."*

The Gift of Connection

As Tom continued rebuilding his relationships, he noticed a profound shift in his emotional well-being. The loneliness that had once consumed him began to fade, replaced by a sense of purpose and belonging.

"It's like I'm part of something again," he said. *"I'm not just existing—I'm living."*

Tom's story is a testament to the resilience of relationships. No matter how much time has passed or how distant things may feel, there's always a way back. It starts with a willingness to show up, to be vulnerable, and to prioritize connection over fear.

If you're feeling distant from loved ones, take a page from Tom's journey. Start small, but start. Send a text, make a call, or write a letter. Focus on listening and showing genuine interest. And remember, it's never too late to rebuild the bridges that matter most.

Because at the end of the day, the legacy we leave isn't about what we accomplish—it's about the love we share and the connections we nurture along the way.

The Art of Connection

The cafe was bustling with life—clinking coffee cups, soft murmurs of conversation, and the hum of an espresso machine in the background. Tom was seated by the window, hands wrapped around a steaming cup of tea as he stared outside. Across from him sat his son, Eric, whose gaze darted between his phone and the street.

Tom had been waiting for this moment. It wasn't easy to ask his son out for coffee, especially with the fear of rejection lurking in the back of his mind. But Eric had agreed, and here they were. Now, the hard part began: connecting.

"So, how's work?" Tom ventured.

Eric looked up briefly. *"Busy,"* he replied, his tone clipped.

The silence that followed felt like an ocean between them. Tom's mind raced for the right thing to say, but nothing came. He sighed quietly, thinking, *How did we get so far apart?*

Recognizing Emotional Bids

What Tom didn't realize in that moment was that Eric had already made an emotional bid—a small, subtle attempt to connect. John Gottman, one of the foremost researchers on relationships, calls these *"emotional bids."* They can be as simple as a comment, a sigh, or even a glance. Responding to these bids, whether by acknowledging them or engaging further, is the foundation of meaningful relationships.

When Eric said *"Busy,"* it wasn't just a throwaway comment. It was a door cracked open, a chance for Tom to step through and say, *"What's been keeping you busy? Tell me more."*

Responding to bids doesn't require grand gestures—it's about showing up in the little moments. Whether it's a smile, a nod, or a question, these small acts send the message: *I see you. I'm here for you.*

The Power of Active Listening

During their next meeting, Tom decided to try something new: active listening. Inspired by what he'd learned about rebuilding relationships, he focused on truly hearing his son instead of thinking about how to respond.

"So, I've been working on this new project," Eric started cautiously, sharing details about a complex software launch.

Instead of jumping in with advice or trying to relate it to his own experiences, Tom simply said, *"That sounds like a lot of responsibility. How are you managing it?"*

Eric hesitated, then relaxed into the conversation. *"It's a lot,"* he admitted. *"But I've been getting better at delegating. My team's great."*

For the first time in years, their conversation flowed naturally. By listening without judgment or the intent to reply, Tom created a safe space for Eric to share.

Active listening is one of the most powerful tools for connection. It requires presence, patience, and a genuine curiosity about the other person's thoughts and feelings. It's not about agreeing or offering solutions—it's about understanding.

Here's how to practice active listening:

1. **Focus Fully**: Put away distractions and give your full attention to the other person.
2. **Reflect**: Repeat back what you've heard, not word for word, but in a way that shows you're engaged. For example, *"It sounds like you're really proud of your team."*
3. **Validate**: Acknowledge their feelings, even if you don't agree with their perspective. Statements like, *"That must be tough"* or *"I can see why you feel that way"* go a long way.

Love, Connection, and Growth

As Tom deepened his relationship with Eric, he began to notice how much he craved these moments of connection. It wasn't just about fixing the past—it was about fulfilling a fundamental human need.

Tony Robbins describes six human needs that drive our behavior, two of which—love/connection and growth—are essential for building deep, meaningful relationships.

1. **Love/Connection**: Humans are wired for connection. We seek relationships that make us feel seen, valued, and loved. For Tom, reconnecting with Eric wasn't just about healing their bond—it was about rediscovering his own need for connection.
2. **Growth**: Relationships thrive when both people are growing, individually and together. As Tom embraced vulnerability and made consistent efforts to connect, he found himself growing in ways he hadn't expected.

"I used to think I had to have all the answers," he told me during one of our sessions. *"But now I see that being present, being real, is what really matters."*

The Role of Vulnerability

Rebuilding relationships requires vulnerability—a willingness to let down your guard and show your true self. For Tom, this meant acknowledging his mistakes and sharing his hopes for the future.

One evening, during a quiet moment at Eric's apartment, Tom said, *"I know I wasn't always there for you the way I should have been. I let work get in the way. But I want to do better. I want to be part of your life, if you'll let me."*

Eric didn't respond right away. But then he nodded, his eyes softening. *"I'd like that too, Dad."*

Vulnerability is scary because it opens the door to rejection. But it's also what makes connection possible. It says, *I'm willing to take the risk because you matter to me.*

Building Lasting Bonds

Over time, Tom's efforts paid off. He and Eric began meeting more regularly, not out of obligation but out of a shared desire to connect. Their conversations grew deeper, filled with laughter, honesty, and mutual respect.

Tom also started applying these principles with other relationships, reaching out to his daughter, Claire, and reconnecting with old friends. Each small step—answering an emotional bid, practicing active listening, embracing vulnerability—built a stronger foundation for connection.

Practical Steps for Deepening Connection

If you're ready to strengthen your relationships, here are some steps inspired by Tom's journey:

1. **Recognize Emotional Bids**: Pay attention to the small ways people try to connect with you and respond with presence and care.
2. **Practice Active Listening**: Focus on understanding, not replying. Validate their feelings and reflect what you hear.

3. **Embrace Vulnerability**: Be honest about your feelings and intentions, even if it feels uncomfortable.
4. **Prioritize Consistent Effort**: Relationships are built in the everyday moments. Show up regularly, even in small ways.

Tom's journey is a reminder that connection isn't about grand gestures—it's about the little things we do every day to show up for the people we love.

As he discovered, it's never too late to rebuild relationships and deepen bonds. It starts with recognizing the power of small moments and committing to the art of connection.

Because the greatest legacy we leave isn't in what we achieve—it's in the love we share and the connections we nurture along the way.

Tom's Steps to Reconnection

Tom stood at his kitchen counter, pen in hand, staring at a blank piece of paper. The room was quiet, save for the soft ticking of the clock on the wall. He had thought this would be easier—just a letter to his kids, letting them know he loved them and wanted to reconnect. But as he sat there, the weight of years of missed moments held him back.

Finally, he began to write.

"Dear Eric and Claire,

I know it's been a while since I really told you how much you mean to me. Life has a way of pulling us in different directions, and somewhere along the way, I let the busyness get in the way of what truly matters—our family. I want you to know how proud I am of you both, and how much I'd like to be a bigger part of your lives moving forward. If you're open to it, I'd love to hear more about what's going on with you and find ways to spend more time together.

With love,

Dad"

As he folded the letters and placed them into envelopes, he felt a flicker of hope. It wasn't perfect, but it was a start.

Small, Intentional Steps

Reconnection often begins with small, deliberate actions. For Tom, that first step was writing to his children—a tangible expression of his love and desire to rebuild their relationship.

When Eric and Claire received their letters, their responses were cautious but warm. *"Thanks for reaching out, Dad,"* Eric texted. *"Let's grab coffee next week."* Claire called him, her voice tinged with surprise but kindness. *"This was really sweet, Dad. I'd like to catch up sometime."*

Encouraged by their openness, Tom began taking other intentional steps. He started scheduling regular phone calls with his kids, not just on holidays but as part of their everyday lives. Each conversation brought them a little closer, revealing shared memories and new ways to connect.

Rebuilding Friendships

With his confidence growing, Tom decided to reconnect with old friends as well. One of his first calls was to Peter, a college buddy he hadn't spoken to in years. *"I was nervous,"* Tom admitted. *"What if he didn't want to hear from me?"*

But when Peter answered, his voice was filled with warmth. *"Tom! It's been ages. I'm so glad you called."*

That phone call turned into a coffee date, which turned into a monthly tradition. Soon, Tom was reconnecting with other friends, creating new shared experiences like game nights and hiking trips.

"I didn't realize how much I missed this," he said one evening, laughing over a board game with friends. *"It feels good to belong again."*

Transforming Relationships

As Tom's efforts grew, so did the transformation in his relationships. His children began reaching out to him, sharing details about their lives and even seeking his advice. *"It's like we're finally a family again,"* Tom said, his voice brimming with emotion.

His friendships deepened as well. Regular meetups and shared experiences created bonds that felt stronger than ever. *"It's not about the time we lost,"* Peter told him one evening. *"It's about the time we have now."*

For Tom, these connections brought a sense of joy and purpose he hadn't felt in years. He no longer woke up feeling alone—he felt part of something bigger, surrounded by people who cared about him.

Practical Tools for Reconnection

Rebuilding relationships doesn't happen overnight, but it becomes possible with consistent effort and the right tools. Here are some practical strategies inspired by Tom's journey:

1. **Write a Heartfelt Letter**: Sometimes, the written word can express emotions that are hard to say out loud. Write a letter to a loved one, sharing your feelings and your desire to reconnect.
2. **Create a Connection Calendar**: Schedule regular time with loved ones, whether it's a weekly phone call, a monthly coffee date, or a family dinner. Consistency builds trust and deepens bonds.
3. **Host Shared Experiences**: Plan activities that bring people together, like game nights, hikes, or shared hobbies. These moments create new memories and strengthen relationships.
4. **Use Conversation Starters:**

Deepen your dialogue with thoughtful questions, like:

"What's been the best part of your week so far?"

"What's something you've always wanted to try?"

"What's a memory of us that makes you smile?"

A Legacy of Love

Tom's story is a testament to the power of small steps. By reaching out, showing up, and prioritizing connection, he transformed his relationships and rebuilt a sense of belonging.

"Life isn't about perfection," Tom said during one of our final conversations. *"It's about presence. It's about being there for the people who matter most."*

As you reflect on your own relationships, consider this: What small step can you take today to deepen your connection with someone you love? Whether it's a phone call, a letter, or simply listening with an open heart, every action brings you closer to a life rich with love and connection.

Because the greatest legacy we leave isn't found in achievements or possessions—it's found in the relationships we nurture and the love we share along the way.

CHAPTER 9:
YOUR SECOND ACT STARTS NOW

Jack's Bold Reinvention

Jack sat in the driver's seat of his car, staring blankly at the dashboard. His suit jacket lay rumpled on the passenger seat, and his tie was already loosened. He had just come from a meeting that confirmed what he had feared for months: his position as a sales executive was being eliminated as part of a corporate downsizing.

After 30 years of climbing the ladder, securing contracts, and hitting targets, it was over. Jack had always been the first to volunteer for the big pitches, the one with a confident handshake and an easy smile. But now, at 57, he felt like a relic of the past.

"How did I get here?" he whispered, gripping the steering wheel. *"And what am I supposed to do now?"*

Defined by the Past

In the weeks that followed, Jack felt aimless. He spent his mornings scrolling job boards, only to close his laptop in frustration. *"Who's going to hire a guy my age?"* he thought. Even the job descriptions felt alien—filled with buzzwords and tech skills he didn't have.

At home, things weren't much better. His wife, Laura, tried to be supportive, but Jack often snapped at her out of frustration. *"I'm just trying to help,"* she said one evening after suggesting he attend a networking event.

"Well, maybe I don't want your help!" he snapped back, immediately regretting his words. Laura left the room, and Jack sank into the couch, feeling like he was letting everyone down.

But what Jack struggled with most wasn't the loss of his job—it was the loss of his identity. For decades, his career had been his anchor, his source of pride and purpose. Without it, he felt adrift, unsure of who he was or what he had to offer.

The Fear of Starting Over

Jack's fears weren't just about finding a new job—they were about how he saw himself. He worried about what his peers would think if they knew he wasn't working. He imagined their pitying looks and whispered conversations: *"Poor Jack. Guess he couldn't keep up."*

Even his family felt like a mirror reflecting his insecurities. His son, Mark, was thriving as a software engineer, and his daughter, Emily, was finishing medical school. Jack had always been proud of their accomplishments, but now he couldn't shake the feeling that he was falling short in their eyes.

"I used to be the one they looked up to," he confided to a friend over coffee. *"Now I'm just the guy who used to have a great job."*

Jack's story is one that resonates with many people navigating midlife. When external roles—like a job title—change, it can leave us questioning our worth and purpose.

The truth is, we often define ourselves by what we do rather than who we are. When those roles shift, it's easy to feel lost, as if we're standing on shaky ground. But midlife isn't just an ending—it's an opportunity to rewrite the narrative, to discover new ways of living with purpose and fulfillment.

As Jack sat with these feelings, he began to realize something important: the skills and experiences that had made him successful in his career hadn't disappeared. They were still part of who he was. And maybe, just maybe, they could be the foundation for something new.

A Flicker of Possibility

One morning, Jack found himself flipping through an old journal he'd kept in his 20s. Amid the notes about work and goals, he found a page where he'd written about his dream of teaching. *"Someday,"* he had written, *"I'd love to help others grow and succeed."*

That word—*someday*—stuck with him. When had he stopped dreaming about *someday*?

That afternoon, he called Laura into the living room. *"I've been thinking,"* he said hesitantly. *"What if I tried something new? Something completely different?"*

Laura's eyes lit up. *"Jack, I think that's exactly what you need."*

The Beginning of a Second Act

Jack's decision to explore teaching wasn't immediate or easy. It took time to find the right fit, but eventually, he started mentoring small business owners through a local community program. At first, he felt out of place, unsure if his corporate experience was relevant to their struggles. But as he shared stories of navigating challenges and building relationships, he saw how his knowledge could make a difference.

"I realized I still have something to offer," Jack said. *"It's just in a different way than before."*

As Jack leaned into this new chapter, he found a sense of purpose that felt deeper than the pride he'd felt in his sales career. He wasn't just closing deals—he was opening doors for others, helping them find their own paths to success.

Reflecting on Identity and Purpose

Jack's journey is a powerful reminder that our identity isn't tied to a job title or a single chapter of our lives. It's something we carry with us, shaped by our experiences, values, and the impact we have on others.

For Jack, midlife wasn't an ending—it was a pivot, a chance to rediscover who he was and what mattered most. His fears of starting over didn't disappear overnight, but they became smaller as his confidence grew.

"I used to think my best years were behind me," Jack said one evening. *"But now I see that they're right in front of me. I just needed the courage to take that first step."*

Jack's bold reinvention didn't just change his career—it changed how he saw himself. He no longer felt defined by his past role or limited by his age. Instead, he saw himself as someone with the power to create, to contribute, and to thrive in his second act.

If you're facing a similar crossroads, take heart. The journey to reinvention starts not with answers but with questions:

- What skills and experiences have shaped me?

- What dreams have I left unexplored?
- What kind of impact do I want to make moving forward?

Your second act isn't about leaving the past behind—it's about building on it, using what you've learned to create something meaningful and new.

Because as Jack discovered, it's never too late to start over. And sometimes, starting over is the greatest opportunity of all.

The Framework for Reinvention

Jack sat at the kitchen table, a notebook open in front of him. The pages were blank, save for the faint blue lines stretching endlessly across the paper, daring him to fill them. On the cover, he'd scribbled one word: *Ikigai*.

It was a concept he'd stumbled upon while listening to a podcast about finding purpose. The idea of aligning what he loved, what he was good at, what the world needed, and what could sustain him financially had ignited something within him. It felt like a map—a way to navigate the uncharted waters of his second act.

Discovering Your Ikigai

The Japanese concept of *Ikigai* translates loosely to *"reason for being."* It's a framework that helps align four key elements:

1. **What You Love**: Your passions and interests.
2. **What You're Good At**: Your skills and talents.

3. **What the World Needs**: Ways to contribute to others or solve problems.
4. **What Can Sustain You**: Financial or practical considerations.

As Jack began filling in his notebook, he realized he had never really thought about these elements in harmony before. His career had focused heavily on what he was good at and what paid the bills, but his passions had been left by the wayside.

He wrote:

- **What I Love**: Teaching, storytelling, connecting with people.
- **What I'm Good At**: Communication, problem-solving, motivating others.
- **What the World Needs**: Mentors, leaders, people who inspire growth.
- **What Can Sustain Me**: A balance of meaningful work and financial stability.

Seeing it all laid out gave Jack a sense of clarity he hadn't felt in years. *"This is the intersection I've been missing,"* he thought.

If you're feeling adrift, exploring your *Ikigai* can be a powerful way to find alignment. Ask yourself these questions:

- What activities make you lose track of time?
- What skills do others often compliment you on?
- What problems do you feel drawn to solve?
- What would you do if money weren't an issue?

By connecting these elements, you can uncover a purpose that feels both meaningful and sustainable.

Embracing a Growth Mindset

As Jack reflected on his *Ikigai*, doubts began to creep in. *"But I've never taught a class,"* he thought. *"What if I'm not good enough? What if I fail?"*

These thoughts are the voice of a fixed mindset—a belief that our abilities and potential are set in stone. Carol Dweck, in her groundbreaking work on the growth mindset, reminds us that adaptability and a belief in self-development are the keys to thriving at any stage of life.

A growth mindset isn't about ignoring challenges; it's about viewing them as opportunities to learn and grow. For Jack, that meant shifting his internal dialogue from *"I can't do this"* to *"I can learn how to do this."*

He signed up for a public speaking course at a local community college, determined to build the confidence he needed to teach. *"It was terrifying at first,"* he admitted. *"But with each class, I got better. And that showed me I could still grow."*

Adopting a growth mindset requires:

- **Reframing Failure**: View mistakes as learning opportunities rather than evidence of inadequacy.
- **Embracing Challenges**: Step out of your comfort zone, knowing that growth often comes from discomfort.
- **Believing in Effort**: Recognize that progress is the result of consistent practice and perseverance.

Legacy Goals: What Do You Want to Be Remembered For?

As Jack worked through his reinvention, he began thinking about legacy. It wasn't just about what he wanted to achieve—it was about how he wanted to be remembered.

He thought about his late father, who had always made time to help others, whether it was mentoring young colleagues or volunteering at the local food bank. *"People still talk about how kind and generous he was,"* Jack realized. *"That's the kind of legacy I want to leave."*

Legacy goals are about aligning your actions with the impact you want to make. They encourage you to think beyond yourself and focus on the ways you can contribute to others.

Jack set three legacy goals for his second act:

1. **Mentorship**: Helping young professionals navigate their careers with confidence and integrity.

2. **Family**: Being present and supportive for his children, creating memories that would last long after he was gone.
3. **Community**: Volunteering his time and skills to uplift those around him.

"What do you want to be remembered for?" is a powerful question. It shifts the focus from short-term achievements to long-term impact, guiding your decisions and actions with purpose.

The Link Between Purpose and Fulfillment

Positive psychology teaches us that purpose-driven actions are closely tied to lasting fulfillment. When we align our daily choices with our values and goals, we create a sense of meaning that sustains us through life's challenges.

Jack began noticing this in his own life. As he mentored young entrepreneurs and reconnected with his children, he felt a renewed sense of vitality. The doubts and fears that had once held him back grew quieter, replaced by a steady confidence in the path he was forging.

"I used to think fulfillment was about hitting milestones," he said. *"But now I see it's about living in alignment with what matters most."*

Practical Tools for Reinvention

If you're ready to embrace your second act, here are some tools to guide you:

1. **Explore Your Ikigai:** Create a diagram with four circles representing what you love, what you're good at, what the world needs, and what can sustain you. Identify where these elements overlap.
2. **Adopt a Growth Mindset:** Challenge limiting beliefs by reframing failures as learning opportunities. Seek out new skills or experiences that stretch your comfort zone.
3. **Define Your Legacy Goals:** Reflect on the impact you want to have on others and write down three specific ways you can start creating that legacy today.
4. **Align Daily Actions with Values:** Use a journal to track how your daily activities reflect your core values and long-term goals.

The Courage to Begin

Jack's journey is a testament to the power of reinvention. By exploring his *Ikigai*, embracing a growth mindset, and setting legacy goals, he transformed his doubts into determination and his fears into fuel.

Your second act is waiting. It doesn't require perfection—just the courage to begin. As you take your first steps, remember that each choice you make is a brushstroke on the canvas of your legacy. And the picture you create has the power to inspire not just your own life, but the lives of those around you.

Jack's Journey to a Second Act

The scent of freshly cut wood filled the small workshop, mingling with the hum of an electric saw and the rhythmic tap of a hammer. Jack stood at his workbench, running his hand over the smooth surface of a coffee table he had just finished. The table wasn't perfect—there was a slight unevenness in one corner—but it was a testament to something greater. It marked the beginning of his second act.

For decades, Jack had dreamed of getting back into woodworking. As a young man, he had spent hours in his grandfather's shed, learning how to craft shelves, birdhouses, and even a small canoe. But as his corporate career took off, his tools gathered dust in the garage. Life had other priorities—or so he thought.

Reconnecting with a Forgotten Passion

It started with a simple project. One day, Jack decided to build a small bookshelf for his daughter, Emily, who had recently moved into a new apartment. He dusted off his tools, bought a stack of pinewood planks, and spent the weekend reacquainting himself with the craft.

"I forgot how much I loved this," he said, stepping back to admire his work. The bookshelf wasn't perfect, but it was functional—and Emily loved it. Soon, her friends were asking if Jack could make pieces for them, too.

"I just wanted to do something small," Jack admitted. *"But once I started, I couldn't stop."*

Woodworking became more than a hobby—it became a way for Jack to reconnect with himself. The act of creating something tangible with his hands brought a sense of calm and purpose he hadn't felt in years.

Turning Passion into Purpose

As word spread about Jack's woodworking, more requests came in. Neighbors, friends, and even acquaintances began asking for custom furniture. What started as a personal project turned into a side business. Jack named it *Second Act Woodworks*, a nod to his journey of reinvention.

But it wasn't just about the furniture. As Jack gained confidence in his craft, he realized he had something even more valuable to share: his knowledge and experience. He started offering woodworking classes at a local community center, teaching young men the skills his grandfather had passed down to him.

"These kids remind me of myself," Jack said. *"They're eager to learn, and it feels good to give them something they can use—something they can be proud of."*

Mentoring became one of the most fulfilling parts of Jack's second act. He wasn't just teaching woodworking—he was teaching resilience, patience, and the joy of creating something from nothing.

Regaining Confidence and Identity

Jack's journey wasn't without its challenges. There were moments of doubt, especially in the early days of his business. *"What if no one wants what I'm making?"* he wondered. *"What if I fail?"*

But each piece he completed, each student he mentored, chipped away at those fears. Slowly, Jack began to see himself not as a man defined by his past career, but as someone capable of growth and reinvention.

"I used to think my value was tied to my title," he said. *"Now I see that it's about what I contribute—not just to myself, but to others."*

Jack's second act wasn't just about building furniture—it was about building a life that aligned with his values. He found joy in the process, pride in his work, and a sense of purpose in the impact he was making on his community.

Practical Tools for Your Second Act

If Jack's journey resonates with you, consider these tools to help you craft your own second act:

1. **Ikigai Diagram**

    - Create a diagram with four circles representing:

        - What you love
        - What you're good at
        - What the world needs
        - What can sustain you

Identify where these circles overlap to uncover your *"reason for being."*

2. **Legacy Planner Worksheet**

    - Reflect on what you want to be remembered for. Write down three ways you can start aligning your daily actions with your legacy goals.

3. **Action Plan Template**

    - Break down your vision into actionable steps:
        - Start small (e.g., complete one project, take a class).
        - Build momentum (e.g., share your work, seek feedback).

- Scale with purpose (e.g., turn a passion into a side business or community project).

A Life Aligned with Values

As Jack's journey shows, your second act isn't about reinventing the wheel—it's about rediscovering what makes you feel alive and finding ways to share it with the world.

"Every piece I make, every student I teach, it's a reminder that it's never too late to start over," Jack said. *"This isn't just a second act—it's the best act."*

Your second act is waiting. Whether it's a long-lost passion, a new skill, or a desire to make an impact, the path forward begins with one step. Like Jack, you have the tools within you to create a life that reflects your best self—one that leaves a legacy of love, purpose, and joy.

Because the greatest acts of our lives aren't the ones we've already lived—they're the ones we choose to create next.

Conclusion:
Your New Beginning Awaits

Your Journey to Transformation

As you turn the final pages of this book, I want to pause and reflect on the incredible journey we've taken together. From rediscovering forgotten dreams to reigniting passion in relationships, reclaiming vitality, and building a life of purpose, this book was designed to be more than just words on a page—it was meant to be a guide, a companion, and a source of encouragement as you embraced your second act.

A Journey of Reinvention

We began by challenging the notion that it's ever *"too late."* Together, we explored how aging is not a limitation but an opportunity to harness wisdom, experience, and the lessons of the past to create something extraordinary.

In *Part 1: Reignite Your Inner Fire,* we tackled fears of wasted time and limiting beliefs. You learned how to reconnect with forgotten passions and dreams, unlocking a sense of vitality and hope that perhaps had been lying dormant.

In *Part 2: Build the Life You've Always Wanted,* we delved into actionable strategies for improving your health, reigniting love and connection, and taking charge of your finances. Through relatable stories and practical tools, we aimed to equip you with the mindset and habits needed to create meaningful, lasting change.

Finally, in *Part 3: Leave Your Mark and Live Fully,* we focused on legacy and connection. Together, we explored the importance of aligning daily actions with values, deepening bonds with loved ones, and finding fulfillment by living with purpose.

Have You Reached Your Goals?

This book wasn't just about ideas—it was about action. So now, I ask you to reflect:

- Have you taken steps to reignite your passions and embrace new opportunities?
- Are you prioritizing your health, relationships, and financial confidence in ways that feel meaningful?
- Do you feel more connected to your purpose and the legacy you want to leave behind?

If the answer is *"yes,"* then I hope this book has served as a catalyst for transformation. And if you're still on the path, that's okay, too—growth is a lifelong journey. What matters most is that you've taken the first steps.

Gratitude for Your Time

To be here, at this point in the book, means you've invested something incredibly valuable: your time. For that, I am deeply grateful. In a world full of distractions, choosing to focus on self-discovery and personal growth is an act of courage and commitment.

Your willingness to reflect, learn, and take action inspires me, and it's been an honor to walk this journey with you.

A Small Request

If this book has resonated with you, I humbly ask for your feedback. Leaving a review on Amazon not only helps me understand what worked for you but also supports the creation of more books like this one. Your voice matters, and it's through your experiences that I can continue to grow and serve.

If this book has made a difference in your life, even in a small way, please share your thoughts. And if you think someone you know could benefit from these pages, pass it along. Together, we can create a ripple effect of transformation and hope.

The Next Chapter of Your Life

This book may be ending, but your journey is just beginning. You have the tools, the mindset, and the courage to step boldly into your second act. Embrace it with determination, curiosity, and the knowledge that the best is yet to come.

Thank you for allowing me to be part of your story. Now, go write the next chapter. It's yours to create.

Bibliography

Below is a list of references, concepts, and resources mentioned or drawn upon during the development of this book. These works have been acknowledged to ensure proper credit is given to the authors and thought leaders whose insights have shaped various sections of this text:

Books and Authors Referenced

- **David Bach**: Financial freedom and practical saving insights inspired by:
    - *The Latte Factor: Why You Don't Have to Be Rich to Live Rich*. Atria Books, 2019.
- **John C. Bogle**: Foundational investing principles drawn from:
    - *The Little Book of Common Sense Investing: The Only Way to Guarantee Your Fair Share of Stock Market Returns*. Wiley, 2017.
- **Brené Brown**: Courage, vulnerability, and leadership insights influenced by:

    - *Daring Greatly: How the Courage to Be Vulnerable Transforms the Way We Live, Love, Parent, and Lead*. Gotham Books, 2012.
    - *Dare to Lead: Brave Work. Tough Conversations. Whole Hearts*. Random House, 2018.
- **Gary Chapman**: Relationship dynamics based on:
    - *The 5 Love Languages: The Secret to Love That Lasts*. Northfield Publishing, 2015.
- **James Clear**: Habit formation and growth strategies influenced by:
    - *Atomic Habits: An Easy & Proven Way to Build Good Habits & Break Bad Ones*. Avery, 2018.
- **Dr. Carol Dweck**: Growth mindset principles drawn from:
    - *Mindset: The New Psychology of Success*. Random House, 2006.
- **Tim Ferriss**: Fear-setting and goal redefinition based on:
    - *Why You Should Define Your Fears Instead of Your Goals*. TED Talk, 2017.
- **Viktor Frankl**: Insights on purpose and meaning inspired by:
    - *Man's Search for Meaning*. Beacon Press, 2006.
- **Héctor García & Francesc Miralles**: Life purpose and alignment influenced by:
    - *Ikigai: The Japanese Secret to a Long and Happy Life*. Penguin Books, 2017.

- **Dr. John Gottman & Julie Schwartz Gottman**: Relational principles and emotional connection informed by:
    - *The Eight Dates: Essential Conversations for a Lifetime of Love*. Workman Publishing, 2017.
    - *The Seven Principles for Making Marriage Work: A Practical Guide from the Country's Foremost Relationship Expert*. Harmony Books, 2015.
- **Jeffrey Hirsch**: Seasonal investment patterns and financial insights based on:
    - *Stock Trader's Almanac 2023*. Wiley, 2022.
- **Peter Lynch & John Rothchild**: Practical investing strategies inspired by:
    - *One Up on Wall Street: How to Use What You Already Know to Make Money in the Market*. Simon & Schuster, 2000.
- **Dr. Esther Perel**: Relational dynamics and emotional fidelity discussed in:
    - *The State of Affairs: Rethinking Infidelity*. Harper, 2017.
- **Dave Ramsey**: Financial principles and budgeting insights based on:
    - *The Total Money Makeover: A Proven Plan for Financial Fitness*. Thomas Nelson, 2003.
- **Dr. John Ratey & Eric Hagerman**: Mind-body connection insights informed by:

  - *Spark: The Revolutionary New Science of Exercise and the Brain*. Little, Brown and Company, 2008.
- **Tony Robbins**: Strategies for growth, financial mastery, and energy management inspired by:
  - *Awaken the Giant Within: How to Take Immediate Control of Your Mental, Emotional, Physical, and Financial Destiny*. Simon & Schuster, 2001.
  - *Unlimited Power: The New Science of Personal Achievement*. Simon & Schuster, 1991.
  - *Money: Master the Game: 7 Simple Steps to Financial Freedom*. Simon & Schuster, 2014.
- **Martin Seligman**: Positive psychology and fulfillment principles influenced by:
  - *Flourish: A Visionary New Understanding of Happiness and Well-Being*. Free Press, 2011.
- **Simon Sinek**: Purpose-driven action and leadership insights inspired by:
  - *Start with Why: How Great Leaders Inspire Everyone to Take Action*. Penguin Books, 2009.

Articles and Online Resources

- **Psychology Today**: Practical psychology concepts drawn from articles such as:

- *How Cognitive Distortions Fuel Anxiety.*
- *It's Never Too Late to Change Your Life.*
- *The Power of Hobbies.*

Acknowledgments

The ideas in this book have also been shaped by countless conversations, reflections, and personal experiences. While some concepts are broadly recognized and not attributed to a specific source, they reflect timeless wisdom and practical strategies for living with faith, purpose, and passion.

This bibliography honors the foundational works and contributions that have influenced this book's creation, ensuring readers have a path to explore these resources further for deeper study and understanding.

Made in United States
Orlando, FL
28 June 2025

62376687R00098